T... P... ... ...

Le... ...ed appreciation

Owen & Reta U.

*Pastor*..**Be**
# Encouraged!

# Pastor...Be Encouraged!

## Insights for Maintaining Spiritual Victory

### C. NEIL STRAIT

Beacon Hill Press of Kansas City
Kansas City, Missouri

Copyright 1996
by Beacon Hill Press of Kansas City

ISBN 083-411-6588

Printed in the
United States of America

Cover design: Mike Walsh
Cover photo: Natural Selection Stock Photography Inc.

**Library of Congress Cataloging-in-Publication Data**
Strait, C. Neil
    Pastor—be encouraged! / C. Neil Strait.
        p.   cm.
    Includes bibliographical references.
    ISBN (invalid) 0-8341-1655-8 (pbk.)
    1. Clergy—Prayer-books and devotions, English.   2. Clergy—Job stress.   I. Title.
BV4398.S73   1996                                            96-46406
248.8'92—dc21                                                      CIP

10   9   8   7   6   5   4   3   2   1

To pastors—
who labor in the trenches,
who get muddied in the battle,
who walk through the dark moments with people,
who preach to broken hearts,
who bleed when sin rips homes apart,
who respond to the early morning calls for help,
who comfort hearts when death takes a loved one,
who stand tall when others are small,
who ignite the hopes of a wayward heart,
who feel the crushing hurt of a disappointed mother or
father,
who bear the pain of misunderstanding,
who feel the hurt of rejection,
who give so much—that others might have Jesus,
and hope,
and life!

# CONTENTS

## Life Is a Learning Experience

## You Are God's Responsibility

# Foreword

*May our Lord Jesus Christ himself and God our Father,*
*who loved us and by his grace gave us eternal*
*encouragement and good hope, encourage your hearts*
*and strengthen you in every good deed and word.*
—2 Thess. 2:16-17

GIVEN OPPORTUNITY TO BE EDITOR OF TIIE *PREACH-er's Magazine*, I soon decided that I hoped to leave two distinguishing marks upon my watch as editor.

*First*, I hoped to emphasize the importance of preaching as our high calling. Many magazines and contemporary religious writers talk of the importance of everything else. I believe preaching stands as the top priority for the man or woman called by God and deserves our highest efforts. Proper biblical preaching nourishes the entire Body of Christ, and that is necessary for a healthy church.

*Second*, I hoped to emphasize encouragement to pastors. Anyone having any degree of exposure to pastors today soon realizes they face unparalleled pressures. Discouragement like a low-lying fog creeps into the lowest points of a pastor's experience. He or she feels pushed in so many directions—and for many of the demands faced, he or she has had no formal preparation. Pastors may need some prods, but most of them need encouragement.

In sharing my thoughts with C. Neil Strait, a seminary classmate and longtime friend, we decided to make a special section in the *Preacher's Magazine* titled "Pastor, Be Encouraged." With strong pastoral experience and proven leadership as a district superintendent, as well as being a gifted writer, Dr. Strait took on this assignment. His words of encouragement did not come out as some passive oil poured on troubled waters. Indeed not! He dealt with the things pastors face and feel, but always in the context of practical steps to take toward solutions. Each issue of the *Preacher's Magazine* has been enhanced with Dr. Strait's keen insight and words of uplift and instruction. Apparently his work touched the hearts and hurts of many pastors. Their responses have expressed appreciation for his sensitivity, gratitude for the help he offered, and assurance that we were meeting a felt need.

With joy I commend the publishing of this pertinent and powerful collection from the writing of C. Neil Strait. I congratulate him for taking the time and effort to share his knowledge and wisdom with a wide audience of readers. The literature for God's servants across the world will be richer by this publishing event. I highly recommend it for every pastor everywhere.

—*Randal E. Denny*
Editor, *Preacher's Magazine*

# *Introduction*

FOR NEARLY 16 YEARS GOD HAS GIVEN ME THE PRIVI-
lege of working with pastors. It has been a rewarding and re-
vealing journey. Because I pastored for 19 years, I know
something of the joys and sorrows of the shepherd. Certainly
the pastor's job has not gotten any easier. Facts are, it is more
complex, more demanding, sometimes more or less rewarding, and without doubt more stressful.

In this busy, complex age, pastors need encouragement. Far too many get far too little of it. While I am convinced that 95 percent or more of Christian laypersons
want to encourage their pastors, some get caught up in the
activities and busyness of the church and neglect to do it.
Thank God, there are a host of laypersons who are great
encouragers. They do it well and do it often.

*Pastor . . . Be Encouraged* is written to all who live out
their mission of ministry in the pastorate or who give
themselves to evangelism, staff ministry, chaplaincy, or
parachurch ministry. All are in ministry and know the joys
and heartaches of ministering to and serving people. It is
written with a hope—and a deep prayer—that something
within these pages will speak a word of encouragement or
light (again) the fires of ministry.

One is always indebted to others in any writing assignment. My special thanks to Rev. Randal Earl Denny,
editor of the *Preacher's Magazine,* for allowing me to share
some of these chapters in a column titled "Pastor, Be Encouraged." My thanks to Christine Freed for her secretarial
skills and for her work in typing the manuscript for this
book. My sincere thanks to those pastors whom I serve, for
their allowing me to be a part of their lives and their ministry. There is no higher privilege!

Remember, as you read and as you labor in the vineyard: you are God's responsibility! He has called you, He will nurture you, and He will be with you in the battles of your life. Hear again His promise: "I am with you always, to the very end of the age" (Matt. 28:20). It is a word to you from Him.

# YOU MAKE
# A DIFFERENCE

# 1

# Keep Your Perspective

*For you created my inmost being; you knit me together
in my mother's womb. I praise you because I am fearfully
and wonderfully made; your works are wonderful, I know
that full well. My frame was not hidden from you when I
was made in the secret place. When I was woven together
in the depths of the earth, your eyes saw my unformed
body. All the days ordained for me were written in your
book before one of them came to be.*
—Ps. 139:13-16

MOTHER TERESA HAS SPENT A LIFETIME ENCOUR-
aging people. We can learn from this Nobel peace prize re-
cipient, who said,

> In our efforts to listen to God's words to us, we often
> neglect what might be called his "first word" to us. This is
> the gift of ourselves to ourselves: our existence, our nature,
> our personal history, our uniqueness, our identity. All that
> we have, and indeed our very existence, is one of the
> unique and never-to-be-repeated ways God has chosen to
> express himself in space and time.[1]

Every pastor must keep in perspective the fact that
God has uniquely gifted and called him or her into ministry. The call of a sovereign God is reason to celebrate and
a source from which to draw strength in the hard times.

Criticism can erode this sense of uniqueness and personal style. It can be devastating, discouraging, and disrup-
tive. Mother Teresa's words were written for such situations.

Pastor, keep in mind that no one is the final word—or even the best word—on your ministry. Criticism all too often is a spin-off from what the critic is feeling or the backlash from some conflict he or she is experiencing. Such criticism is not valid.

Your response to the unwarranted and invalid critic should be one of caution and composure. Do not let it erode the person God made you to be. Overreacting by changing yourself to satisfy every critic is self-destructive.

Do be careful to properly assess valid criticism. Be objective. There are times when you are wrong. When you are, it is only the better part of integrity—and wisdom—to admit it and learn from it.

After each criticism, consider three things. *First,* is the critic right? If so, change what needs to be changed, and move on with gratitude. Your critic has helped you. *Second,* if the criticism is unfounded or unfair, don't retaliate or argue. Simply bring closure and move on. *Third,* keep in mind during the process your unique gifts and your secure relationship to God. Most of all, remember that God is the best and final word on your ministry.

Be encouraged, pastor! God has called you and will equip you for ministry in a unique and meaningful way. Bring your critics to the altar of your heart, and let the Holy Spirit help you sort out the facts. His Word in our hearts is a soothing oil for healing and help. His confirmation and instruction silence the sting and hurt of the critic.

# 2

# You Make a Difference

*Now Moses was tending the flock of Jethro his father-in-law, the priest of Midian, and he led the flock to the far side of the desert and came to Horeb, the mountain of God. There the angel of the LORD appeared to him in flames of fire from within a bush. Moses saw that though the bush was on fire it did not burn up. So Moses thought, "I will go over and see this strange sight—why the bush does not burn up." When the LORD saw that he had gone over to look, God called to him from within the bush, "Moses! Moses!" And Moses said, "Here I am." "Do not come any closer," God said. "Take off your sandals, for the place where you are standing is holy ground." Then he said, "I am the God of your father, the God of Abraham, the God of Isaac and the God of Jacob." At this, Moses hid his face, because he was afraid to look at God. The LORD said, "I have indeed seen the misery of my people in Egypt. I have heard them crying out because of their slave drivers, and I am concerned about their suffering. So I have come down to rescue them from the hand of the Egyptians and to bring them up out of that land into a good and spacious land, a land flowing with milk and honey—the home of the Canaanites, Hittites, Amorites, Perizzites, Hivites and Jebusites. And now the cry of the Israelites has reached me, and I have seen*

*the way the Egyptians are oppressing them. So now, go.*
*I am sending you to Pharaoh to bring my people*
*the Israelites out of Egypt."*
—Exod. 3:1-10

I READ A STORY OF AN ELDERLY MAN WHO WAS walking along the beach in the early morning hours, picking up starfish and throwing them into the ocean. A young man asked him what he was doing. He answered, "The stranded starfish will die in the morning sun if left on the beach."

The young man responded, "The beach extends for hundreds of miles, and there are millions of starfish. How can what you are doing make any difference?"

The elderly man threw a starfish into the ocean and simply said, "It makes a difference to that one."[1]

You and I need to remember that everything we do makes a difference, in some way, to someone. In the heat of the battle, when our critics have multiplied and the troops seem arrayed against us, we need to consider how we respond. For while our response will matter very little to our critics, it matters a great deal to those who believe in us.

There are times when your task will seem overwhelming. Just the sheer volume of things to do can drain you of energy and deplete your resources. It is then we are tempted to ask, "What difference does it make?" And honestly, many of the tasks may not make much difference at all. But if some task makes a little difference in just one life, then it makes all the difference in the world.

What pastor/preacher has not gone from the pulpit and had moments of doubt about his or her preaching's making any difference at all? But the occasions when affirmations come—a word spoken at the right time, a bit of light that shines through the preaching moment, or a challenge that lifts life—confirm that preaching *does* make a difference. The impact on various individuals in varying degrees validates preaching and sends us back to our study to pray and search for yet another word from the Lord.

Consider the times when negative voices, within or without, remind you of opposition or failure or even petty grievances. These also are times when you may find yourself asking, "What difference does it all make?" But a person always has a greater ministry than he or she realizes. What you do, how you do it, and the reasons you do it will inspire and help many. Your ministry, even at its worst, can make a difference in someone's life and future. Let that thought prevail when you have your back to the wall and your vision for the future is blurred.

Most of us will be involved in ministries in which we are making a difference in lives one at a time, rather than to scores or hundreds of people. Did not Jesus remind us "there is rejoicing in the presence of the angels of God over one sinner who repents" (Luke 15:10)?

Your ministry is touching someone's life, pastor. It is making a difference to someone, even if you do not see confirmation nor hear any words affirming it. This is our confidence as we yield our ministry to Christ!

# 3

# You Are Significant!

*But now, this is what the LORD says—he who created you,*
*O Jacob, he who formed you, O Israel: "Fear not, for I have*
*redeemed you; I have summoned you by name; you are*
*mine. When you pass through the waters, I will be with*
*you; and when you pass through the rivers, they will not*
*sweep over you. When you walk through the fire, you will*
*not be burned; the flames will not set you ablaze. For I am*
*the LORD, your God, the Holy One of Israel,*
*your Savior; I give Egypt for your ransom,*
*Cush and Seba in your stead.*
—Isa. 43:1-3

MARSHALL SHELLEY IN A *LEADERSHIP* MAGAZINE
column shares an observation from an interview with Jack
Hayford, author of the song "Majesty." Hayford tells of
visiting Winston Churchill's boyhood home in Blenheim
Palace in Oxfordshire, England. He described the beauty of
the landscaped grounds. As he walked to his car from the
rose garden, he said to his wife, "In a place this magnifi-
cent, it's easy to see how a person raised here could readily
imagine himself to be a person of destiny. There's something about the environment that makes you feel, 'I am significant.'"

The visit to Churchill's boyhood place left a deep im-
pression on Hayford, and from it came the inspiration for
his song "Majesty." Before Hayford left Oxfordshire, he

said, upon reflection, "I thought about all the majesty and dignity we've been endowed with in Christ. If that would dawn on all God's people, if they would sense their significance in Him, then we all could become more aware of His purpose in us."[1]

Every pastor needs a fresh reminder of his or her significance. Amid all the pressures of pastoral ministry, some of which can erode a pastor's self-image and sense of vision, it is important to be focused on God's purpose in our lives.

How can pastors keep a healthy view of significance and purpose? First and foremost, your time communing with God must have highest priority. While nearly everyone would agree with this priority, all of us know how it can be challenged by the things to do and the many activities that crowd our lives. You cannot love people, as an authentic pastor does, without the claims on your time becoming numerous. The result is a constant challenge to keep spiritually fit and to serve those under your care.

Despite the challenge of time and the claims of people, our time alone with God is the only thing that will prepare us for authentic service to people. Without a time to talk and listen to Him, our significance drains, and our purpose fades. No ministry was created by the Lord to be stretched across the panorama of human needs and to exist by human initiative. Where the Divine is missing as the key ingredient for service, then significance and purpose soon diminish.

Only in the quiet times with God does life see the greater view and feel the touch that enables one to serve with dignity and joy. In Hayford's words, "There's something about the environment that makes you feel, 'I am significant.'" From communion with God, the pastor hears the word he or she needs to hear: "You have been called for a purpose."

Every pastor at some point in ministry comes to crisis, confusion, and criticism. When the barrage of negative assaults come, it is important for the pastor to have had a fresh and current encounter with God. If the pastor goes to work without some word from God ringing in his or her heart, the negatives will erode the joy and dampen the significance of service.

Great painter Leonardo da Vinci was accustomed to long pauses as he painted. When someone inquired about those long pauses, he replied, "When I paused the longest, I made the best strokes."

Pastor, God has a word for your ministry that will encourage, will reignite your significance, and will clarify your purpose. Consider the caution of Quaker Rufus Jones: "Keep a window open on the Godward side."

# 4

# Do the Best You Can

*Whatever you do, work at it with all your heart, as*
*working for the Lord, not for men, since you know that*
*you will receive an inheritance from the Lord as a*
*reward. It is the Lord Christ you are serving.*
—Col. 3:23-24

IN HIS BOOK *STRAIGHT TALK FOR MONDAY MORN-*
*ing,* Allan Cox tells the story of United States Olympic star
Carl Lewis. At the 1984 Olympics in Los Angeles, Lewis
was victor and hero on the United States team and hoped
to repeat his feats in 1988.

The goal of Lewis in the 1988 Olympics was to win the
100-meter sprint and defeat his arch rival, Canada's Ben
Johnson. He had prepared well and went into the
Olympics in Seoul with his mind set on winning. But on
the September day the race was run, Ben Johnson set a
new world record by running the 100 meters in 9.79 sec-
onds. Lewis had to settle for second.*

Lewis set an American record even in defeat. While he
was not always a good loser, his perspective on this occasion was gracious. He said, "I ran the best I could, and now
it's on to the next race." He further added, "The Olympics
is about performing the best you can, and I did."[1]

---

*Johnson was later disqualified from the competition because he tested posi-
tive for steroid usage. Lewis was officially declared the winner.

Pastor, ministry is about performing the best you can! That is all we are responsible for. But we *are* responsible for that. When we can go to sleep at night, knowing we have done our best that day, we can be at peace with ourselves. We can do no more.

What are the benefits of giving one's best?

*One,* you have the approval of God. What more do you need? If you have His approval for ministry, you have inner peace and assurance to face any battle, endure any crisis, or pursue any task. To settle for less is to begin the descent to the lowlands when the inner turmoil increases, relationships deteriorate, and crises build. One way to stay encouraged is to desire the approval of God on your ministry.

*Two,* you have the approval of yourself. Your most discouraging times come when you have not done your best. Your self-esteem is damaged, and your motivation to journey onward is deterred. In such circumstances, pastors become their own worst enemies. Where you are doing battle with yourself, the conflict spreads to other areas of life—your marriage, your ministry, your relationships.

*Three,* you have the approval of those whom you serve. For the most part, people do not want, nor do they expect, perfection. However, they do want, and have the right to expect, that we give our best. Ninety-five percent (or better) of laypersons are gracious, supportive, understanding, and encouraging of their pastor. They go the extra mile more than they are often given credit for. They love their pastor, though they are disappointed when he or she lets them down. But for the pastor who does his or her best, they are waiting to encourage, support, and applaud.

*Four,* you are equipped to face the critics and the crises if you have done your best. Too often individuals who have compromised, be they pastor or layperson, respond out of guilt in the time of crisis. Their self-esteem is low; hence, their security is threatened by criticism. In times of crisis their emotions are churned, and they become defensive instead of operating out of reason. But the desire to do our best is a positive deterrent to the critic and the crisis. Occasionally it seems our best is not enough for some people. When this happens, the assurance in your heart better equips you to answer your critics, resolve the crisis, and move on with meaningful ministry.

*Five,* you are more open to growth, learning, and success when you have done your best. When you commit to do your best, you stretch your mind and heart; you learn new and better ways; and you develop a deep dependence on God. This pursuit enriches your life, expanding its abilities, deepening its character, and broadening its potential. Through such growth processes you are better equipped, not only to give excellence to ministry, but also to have resources for the rough times.

*Six,* you receive the benefits from giving your best in ministry. From such a commitment to excellence, the pastor sees lives changed in exciting ways. Such pastors see growth in those whom they serve, since their pursuit of excellence is a challenge to others.

Pastor, be intent on doing your best in ministry. Give time to preparation, prayer, planning—those activities that will point you toward excellence and equip you for greater ministry. Guard your time so that you give yourself to priority ministry rather than letting the precious moments slip away with trivia and nonessentials. You will find encouragement by giving your best to ministry. Your heart will respond to such service with satisfaction and peace. This is motivation for future ministry and growth.

# 5

# Attitude Is Crucial

*Your attitude should be the same as that of Christ Jesus:
Who, being in very nature God, did not consider equality
with God something to be grasped, but made himself
nothing, taking the very nature of a servant, being made in
human likeness. And being found in appearance as a man,
he humbled himself and became obedient to death—even
death on a cross!*
—Phil. 2:5-8

ATTITUDE IS AN IMPORTANT PART OF LIFE. WHETHER
we are talking about jobs, relationships, or circumstances, attitude always remains a factor. It is an especially important
factor in pastoral ministry. A part of the reason comes from
the fact that no job involves working with volunteers quite
like the ministry does. As ministry changes—and it has over
the last 5 to 10 years—attitude remains the one constant factor.

As any pastor knows, attitude is the one factor that af-
fects morale in the local church—perhaps more than finances, building needs, or a host of other things. It is present as a positive or negative influence in every situation.
Let's consider some major factors about attitude.

*First*, attitudes can be very positive. Every pastor is
grateful for an upbeat, optimistic spirit in his or her people. It makes pastoring a joy and is an encouragement to
the fellowship. Pastor, drink deep from the well of the pos-

itive folk. Be encouraged by their support, their attitude, and their service. Nurture and care for these people, and be careful not to neglect them. Let them know that you appreciate them, and pray that their kind might increase.

*Second,* attitudes at times will be negative and divisive. Every pastor has to deal with this at some time. Negative attitudes can crash-land the best program, sidetrack anything good, and demolish what has taken years to build. These attitudes can be carnal, sinful, and tragic, but often we say too little about them for fear we will hurt someone's feelings. So where a bad-attitude person exists, we tiptoe around him or her, hoping against hope that everything will hold together. Too often the church is held hostage by negative and destructive attitudes.

Negative attitudes have been with the church since its beginning. Nothing you and I do will eliminate them. Develop a strategy to nurture the positive crowd and not always give in to the negative folk. This is easier said than done. But you will gain nothing by allowing negative attitudes to rub off on you or draw you into similar retaliation. Guard against letting pessimism affect your ministry and the ministry of the church. A negative word is never a good word for the church, and certainly it is not the last word.

A crippled boy was asked how he could face life and embrace it when he was so crippled with a disease. The boy replied, "It never touched my heart."

Pastor, don't let negativity touch your heart and spirit.

*Third,* attitudes determine relationships. Years ago I made pastoral arrangements in a church where I thought the incoming pastor was less equipped to serve than the pastor who was leaving. But to my amazement great growth occurred. When I met with the church board during my annual visit, they said to me, "We know he loves us. He cares. He has a great attitude." That had become his entry into their lives, and it gave him a track for effective ministry. While the other pastor was "more qualified," his attitude had kept his talents thwarted and stymied. Pastor, your attitude, if it is caring, loving, positive, and helpful, will enable you to build great relationships with your people.

*Fourth,* right attitudes must always focus on the main purpose. Too often we overlook the primary objective of our ministry because we are caught up in the emotional turmoil of something more trivial.

I heard of a man who went to London to tour the land of Wesley history and to do research in the universities. It was an opportunity of a lifetime! When he came home, though, all he could talk about was the fact that his hotel window in London would not open. He never talked about the great "walks with Wesley" or the beauty of the country. His trip was remembered by a stuck window.

Pastors must guard their reactions to attitudes, people, and events. A thousand things will come along to tempt you to be negative and reactionary, but the mission of your work invites you to look above the current battle, to see the goal of influence, love, care, and ministry.

Ernest Campbell said in one of his books that "it doesn't really matter whether an action is profitable or popular, whether it is practical or realistic, whether it wins a salute from a city or a nation. What matters only and always is whether it can be understood as following Jesus Christ."[1]

So, pastor, love those who may not be lovable, understanding that your "labour of love" is your ministry and that your real strength comes from God and His positive people (1 Thess. 1:3, KJV).

# 6

# One Way to Happiness

*Young men, in the same way be submissive to those who
are older. All of you, clothe yourselves with humility
toward one another, because, "God opposes the proud but
gives grace to the humble." Humble yourselves, therefore,
under God's mighty hand, that he
may lift you up in due time.*
—1 Pet. 5:5-6

THE LATE KARL MENNINGER, THE GREAT PSYCHIA-
trist, was once asked what help he would offer a lonely,
unhappy person. He said, "Lock the door behind you, go
across the street, find someone who is hurting, and help
them."[1]

All of us at some time go through a moment in our
lives when there is crisis and criticism. Unhappiness
knocks at the door. What is a pastor to do?

A number of years ago while in pastoral ministry, I
was going through a rough time. I was trying to juggle a
couple of crises, was working with a staff problem, and
was trying to iron out a misunderstanding between two
friends. While I was sitting at my desk one day, it occurred
to me that what I needed was a change of scenery.

I thought of three people in my congregation who
were going through rough times. One, a youth, had gotten
in trouble with the law. An elderly man had lost substan-
tial money in an investment. Another man had lost his job,

and his self-image was shattered. In one day I went to each
of these and tried to take Jesus into their lives. It was a
long and taxing day. But when I pulled into the garage, just
before midnight, I felt I had done ministry in the name of
Jesus. It was therapy for me.

The next morning after my devotional time, I made a
decision that impacted the remainder of my pastoral ministry. Every Monday, as I began my week, I asked three
questions as I put my week together: (1) Who is hurting
and needing his or her pastor? (2) Who is missing whom I
need to visit? (3) Who needs a word of encouragement? It
revolutionized the way I thought, prayed, and planned. I
felt better about myself and consequently was better able
to handle and deal with problems.

Consider these three observations concerning Menninger's advice:

1. If we focus on problems too long, we develop a
problem syndrome. Negativism creeps in and challenges
any positive possibility.

2. When we focus on others, our own problems seem
small. As I drove home the night after I visited those three
individuals who had deep needs, the problems I was dealing with seemed much smaller than they did the day before.

3. I believe there is a spiritual principle at work when
we are serving, helping others. I think it is a part of our
Lord's words, "Give, and it shall be given unto you" (Luke
6:38, KJV). So many times we interpret this to mean that
money or gain will come to us. I rather think it can be in-
terpreted to mean that God will give us His presence, His
strength, His care.

So, pastor, you may be knee-deep in problems to the
point at which all other possibilities are blocked out. But
maybe what you need to do is "lock the door behind you,
go across the street, find someone who is hurting, and help
them." Remember, when you do, the God of all grace and
comfort goes with you.

# THE CHALLENGE
# OF MINISTRY

# 7

# The Soul of the Church

*Then he called the crowd to him along with his disciples
and said: "If anyone would come after me, he must deny
himself and take up his cross and follow me. For whoever
wants to save his life will lose it, but whoever loses his life
for me and for the gospel will save it."*
—Mark 8:34-35

I READ SOMETHING RECENTLY THAT WAS ENCOUR-
aging. It pointed out that the soul and strength of the
church is in people whose jobs are not prominent or glamorous but who just tough it out, hang in there, ride out the
storms, and cheer the pastor on. Every pastor needs members like this and thanks the Lord frequently when he or
she finds them.

Don McCullough, writing in "Waking from the American Dream," tells a story of Winston Churchill during
World War II. Churchill called labor leaders to a meeting to
enlist their support. At the end of his presentation, he
asked them to picture in their minds a parade he knew
would be held in Piccadilly Circus after the war. First, he
said, would come the sailors who had kept the vital sea-
lanes open. Then would come the soldiers who had come
home from Dunkirk and then gone on to defeat Rommel in
Africa. Then would come the pilots who had driven the
Luftwaffe from the skies.

"Last of all," he said, "would come a long line of

sweat-stained, soot-streaked men in miners' caps. Someone would cry from the crowd, 'And where were you during the critical days of our struggle?' And from ten thousand throats would come the answer, 'We were deep in the earth with our faces to the coal.'"[1]

Now there is nothing glamorous about work that keeps your "face to the coal." It is not the job one seeks on the ladder to prominence. But let it be clear: without the people who keep their "faces to the coal," there is no glamour for anyone else, no prominence—in fact, no Church!

As I look across the Church, more and more I appreciate the people with their "faces to the coal." Without them, we do not raise money for missions or ministry; we do not have revivals; we do not build buildings; we do not raise a pastor's salary. They are the soul and strength of the Church, and someone needs to recognize their hard work and faithfulness.

Pastor, your future and mine depend on the people who have their "faces to the coal." They are the "salt of the earth" people. Because they are busy in the trenches, they do not have time to criticize. Because they are at their tasks, they see every pastor as a shepherd and a partner with them in a great mission.

So, pastor, be encouraged by the people who have their "faces to the coal." They are the real heroes. They look to you for leadership through their sweat-stained eyes. They pray for you, love you, support you. When the bills need to be paid, they pay them. When the budgets need to be raised, they raise them. And then they quietly go back to work, rejoicing and looking for better days.

Look around you, pastor! There are more "faces to the coal" people than there are of the other kind. They are on your side, carrying the load, holding you up in prayer, being Jesus people where it counts. Thank God for them.

# 8

# Good Advice for the Early Years

*Know therefore that the LORD your God is God; he is the faithful God, keeping his covenant of love to a thousand generations of those who love him and keep his commands.*
—Deut. 7:9

ONE OF THE PRIVILEGES WE HAVE AS MEMBERS OF the family of God is being recipients of godly, caring advice. Early in my pastoral ministry I came under severe criticism from a couple in my congregation. It was devastating to me. I turned to a veteran pastor for advice and counsel.

This neighboring pastor, Rev. Bob Weathers, listened to my cry for help. Without agreeing with my critics— which he probably could have done—he listened with empathy and care. I shall never forget his advice to me: "Never let the word of a person be the last word on your ministry." It was just what I needed at that moment. It put my dilemma in perspective and gave me courage to go on.

I have had occasion over the years to draw strength and encouragement from this advice. I have thought a great deal about my friend's statement. Let me share some of my thoughts with you.

*First*, "Never let the word of a person be the last word on your ministry" is good advice because no one has all the facts about whatever it is he or she is criticizing. Often I remind congregations and church boards that the pastor must see the entire church and consider every person in planning, decision making, and responses. But laypersons often see things in one-dimensional ways. With limited knowledge and understanding, a person's idea may or may not be valid.

*Second,* we need to remember that a lot of things can impact a person's view of one's ministry. What I did not understand in those early years—but my mentor knew so well—was that often people have their own agendas. They have dreams too. Often some of our severest critics are good people who want to see the work of God progress as much as we do. So it is easy for good people to interpret a pastor's plan or methods as destroying their dream. Remember that all of us are pursuing the same goal, but down different tracks.

*Third,* remember that often the critical words on a pastor's ministry stem from unprocessed anger, a disappointment, some personal failure, or a heartbreak. Out of such hurts, people lash out at others because the reservoir gets to overflowing. Often these people are mad at God for some event or experience. The one who gets the venom is the pastor, whom people perceive as God's representative. Again, if we can remember that their overflow is not the definitive word about our ministry, we will survive the crossfire.

*Fourth,* remember that some people are critical by nature. I remember an incident that occurred a number of years ago as I was leaving a board meeting where the pastor had been under the gun of a person's attack. It was so shocking, for the church was growing, and all seemed to be going well. The son of the individual attacking the pastor followed me to my car and, with tears in his eyes, said, "Mom is just critical by nature. Please understand. She is a good woman, but it seems she must always find something to criticize. Pray for her." I put my arm around the son, and we prayed together. What a tragic story of so many who have developed the habit of criticism and faultfinding!

*Fifth,* remember that God has the best and final word on your ministry. He has called you into service. He will equip and encourage you to serve, to minister, to love, and to care. It will mean, on occasion, that we will have to bring our fractured self-image to God and let it be bathed in the presence and Word of the One who called and will sustain us.

There will be times when you and I must bring the thoughts and words of our critics to God in order to get His perspective. I think it is always valid for us to ask, "What can we learn from this?" "Does this person have a point?" "Are they right?" God may be saying something to us through the ordeal. It is dangerous to assume that every critic is wrong. Somewhere in the process we must be able to distinguish the bottom line and learn from our worst experiences.

Pastor, a person's word on your ministry is never the final word. Only God's Word and guidance sustains, strengthens, and stretches us for a loving, caring ministry. Thanks, my friend, for advice that has lasted a lifetime.

# 9

# Remember the Joyous Occasions

*Rejoice in the Lord always. I will say it again: Rejoice! Let your gentleness be evident to all. The Lord is near. Do not be anxious about anything, but in everything, by prayer and petition, with thanksgiving, present your requests to God. And the peace of God, which transcends all understanding, will guard your hearts and your minds in Christ Jesus.*
—Phil. 4:4-7

SOMETHING ABOUT MEMORY SEEMS PARADOXICAL. One can remember the sad, the negative, and the failures but so soon forget the joyful, the positive, and the successes. Pastors are no different. The hurts sting a little longer than ordinary experiences, while the joys fade with the onrushing episodes of life.

A good admonition for pastors is to remember the joyous occasions of ministry. Keep them etched on your mind as points of reference. Savor them for the troubled times. Draw inspiration and strength from them when you walk through the tight, tense spots of ministry.

A few months ago I dropped a note of encouragement to a pastor who I knew had gone through some rough weeks. He is a dedicated pastor who has done a terrific job in his church. He cares for people and gives good leadership to his flock. But the financial downturn in his community created a crisis in his church since several had to move away in order to secure jobs. The exodus was taking its toll on the pastor and on his people. I tried to encourage him by my letter, affirming his ministry and efforts.

His response was a letter I will treasure for a long time. "You will never know what your note meant to me," he wrote. "The timing could not have been more perfect. I have put your note in a place where every morning it reminds me that someone cares, believes in me, and affirms my ministry."

As I laid the note on my desk, I paused to pray for this pastor, asking that amid the gloom with which he was working, he would remember the joyful notes of ministry. I prayed that he would remember the young man who had knelt at the altar just a few weeks before, or the good response he had to an innovative ministry, and the note he had shared with me from a man in his church to whom he had ministered.

Every pastor needs to work on remembering the good times of ministry, the joyous occasions, the treasured experiences, the high moments of service. There are victories! God is alive and at work in His Church.

Consider these strategies for ministry that help us keep both the joyous and the unpleasant in perspective:

*First*, do not overlook your devotional and prayer life. No improvement has been found for personal devotions and prayer. One may find better ways to do these spiritual disciplines, but nothing better will replace them. Times of prayer and Bible reading give God an opportunity to put the events and experiences of ministry in perspective. Moments with God give the Holy Spirit occasion to be Paraclete to us—to come alongside us in our endeavors, especially the tough things, and be Helper, Encourager, Enabler, Strengthener—all we need in order to cope with ministry in effective ways. Prayer gives God opportunity to have a part in our ministry.

*Second*, remember that your mental focus determines your attitude. If you focus on all the things that are not working, they can snowball into fear and create near paralysis. The better strategy is to stay positive, to think solutions, to remember that not all is bad. A positive attitude keeps hope alive and nurtures its potential. Every pastor can choose his or her attitude. The choice may determine the future.

*Third*, believe that failure is only part of any story. Refuse to accept failure as the last word. Too often beauty comes out of ashes, success comes out of failure, and joy rises out of sorrow. Keep in your mind and heart a ready reference of the successes. Find a way to cope with failure, to resource its urgings, to forbid it from overtaking you. God invites us to draw upon His resources. Jeremiah's words come as a fresh reminder of this: "Call to me and I will answer you and tell you great and unsearchable things you do not know" (33:3).

What do you choose to remember from ministry this past week or month or year? Cultivate a grateful heart, and keep a ledger of the good. It will become a resource for the hard times.

# 10

# Learning from the Master

*Come to me, all you who are weary and burdened,*
*and I will give you rest. Take my yoke upon you and*
*learn from me, for I am gentle and humble in heart,*
*and you will find rest for your souls. For my yoke is*
*easy and my burden is light.*
—Matt. 11:28-30

JOHN HENRY JOWETT IN ONE OF HIS DEVOTIONALS picks up on the description of Jesus we see in the Gospel of Mark: "He was teaching his disciples" (9:31). Jowett writes, "And my Lord will teach me. He will lead me into 'the deep things' of God. There is only one school for this sort of learning, and an old saint called it the Academy of Love, and it meets in Gethsemane and Calvary, and the Lord Himself is the teacher, and there is room in the school for thee and me."[1]

Life is a learning experience. The privilege we have, as disciples of Jesus, is that He is our Teacher. That means the One who has called us to ministry will also be the One who will teach us how to minister. It is a thought rich with comfort and strength.

What does this mean for us in ministry?

*First,* it means that when failures, mistakes, problems, and crises come our way, it is not the end of the road. Jesus, the Master Teacher, waits to take the failures, the mistakes, the problems, and the crises and be Teacher to us in the midst of these. It is the Lord's way of bringing order out of chaos, beauty from ashes, hope out of despair. This is the history of God—taking the worst, the darkest, the most despairing, and writing a new chapter.

So during the next crisis you have, remember that such becomes the raw material for the Lord's work. Take your turmoil to the Lord, and enroll in His Academy of Love for a course in victory and triumph. He is always ready to lead His children to brighter days and new beginnings.

*Second,* it means all of us are in the fashioning stage. I like the children's song that says, "He's still workin' on me." The secret to personal growth is to let Him be the Teacher. Too often other voices chart our path, and other teachers seem more inviting. For your task of ministry you must make sure that the one Voice you are hearing and the one Teacher you are following is Jesus. When He has your relinquished will and your ready mind, He can do His work in refinement and disciple making.

*Third,* it means that as Teacher, Jesus welcomes our questions, our frustrations, our doubts, because only as one reaches out with these expressions will the truth be found. A good teacher welcomes the inquiring mind, the searching heart, and the one in pursuit of answers. So does Jesus! He welcomes our searching in His Academy of Love, for He is "the way and the truth and the life" (John 14:6).

Jowett closed his devotional thought with this admonition: "They who would be great scholars in this school must become 'as little children.' Through the child-like spirit we attain unto Godlike wisdom."[2]

Pastor, be encouraged! Our Teacher-Shepherd knows the way through the lowlands, and He will lead you to the brighter side, where His truth shines through and His love comforts and binds up the wounds. The lessons in Gethsemane and Calvary are sometimes painful, but they equip us for ministry and service. Those very lessons were modeled by Jesus, and He waits to teach them to us.

# 11

# The Challenge of Ministry

*The Spirit of the Sovereign* LORD *is on me, because the*
LORD *has anointed me to preach good news to the poor. He
has sent me to bind up the brokenhearted, to proclaim
freedom for the captives and release from darkness for the
prisoners, to proclaim the year of the* LORD's *favor and the
day of vengeance of our God, to comfort all who mourn,
and provide for those who grieve in Zion—to bestow on
them a crown of beauty instead of ashes, the oil of gladness
instead of mourning, and a garment of praise instead of a
spirit of despair. They will be called oaks of righteousness, a
planting of the* LORD *for the display of his splendor.*
—Isa. 61:1-3

I DOUBT THERE WAS EVER A TIME WHEN MINISTRY
was easy. Every age and culture has presented a unique set
of challenges for the pastor. But our times may be compli-
cated by things with which no other age has had to con-
tend. H. B. London Jr. and Neil B. Wiseman, writing in
their book *Pastors at Risk,* state:

> Pastoring is harder now than ever before. Unprecedent-
> ed shifts in moral, social and economic conditions are halt-
> ing congregations and bringing into question the way min-
> istry is done. These changing circumstances and values
> directly affect pastors and their way of life. Many pressing
> contemporary difficulties were largely unknown in earlier
> periods of Christian history.[1]

There are two ways we can meet the challenges to ministry: we can react or we can respond. When we react, we set ourselves up for bitterness and failure. But when we respond, we are proactive, creative, and faithful. Let's take a positive look at the challenges.

*Your work is rigorous.* Pastoring isn't easy. As a result, it gives you opportunity to develop, to learn, to stretch, and then be creative. All of these responses are good for an individual and, hence, good for one's ministry. They force you to expand your repertoire of knowledge and expertise. The answers of a few years ago—or even a few weeks ago—are no longer relevant and helpful. You must read, observe, keep up, expand, stretch, if you are to have a fulfilling ministry.

On any given week if you were to list the items calling for your attention, you can make a case, even in the smallest church, for challenges beyond your abilities. The social ills, the abuse factors (mental, physical, sexual), the addictions, the bitterness, the loneliness all call for the pastor's time and expertise. Eugene H. Peterson pictures the scene like this: "We inhabit an atmosphere so full of rush and demand. Pastors practice their craft in the middle of a traffic jam, noisy with people's hurts, dangerous with hurtling ambitions and reckless urgencies, crowded with people intent on getting to their destinations and angrily frustrated when others are impediments in their path."[2]

Pastor, you preach to people every week whose lives are lived out in a monotonous routine. They would gladly trade places with you. You minister to people who must labor every day, doing what they have done for years. They have little or no opportunity to stretch their horizon and expand their minds. They would welcome challenge and the opportunity to have variety. Be thankful for the challenge of your work.

*Your character is tested.* Be thankful for this? Yes. The work of pastoral ministry, or ministry at any level, is a test of our character and integrity. Because of whose we are and the calling He has placed upon our lives, we have a mandate to live holy and wholesome lives. We should do this regardless of our occupation. But because of the unique challenges of ministry, we are tested beyond the ordinary. Such testing can help to keep us alert, sharp, and sensitive.

The challenge to character certainly calls one to keep his or her spiritual life in order. While I am convinced God does not have "more grace" for pastors than anyone else, I am convinced pastors must live with a greater sense of dependency on Him.

New temptations seem to come on line every week. They include temptations to succeed, to make money, to compromise one's moral life, to shade the truth for one's benefit. All of them test the character and integrity of a pastor. When you withstand them, rise above them, and are victorious over them, you are a stronger person and consequently a better pastor.

*Your future in ministry is at stake.* Perhaps the most stressful challenge in ministry is to know that your ministry always seems to be "on the line." Because the pastor is such a public person, there are risks and minefields. The challenge, then, is to pursue ministry with excellence, commitment, and trust. It is not all bad that the pastor has to work each day, knowing that his or her future is at stake. For from the consciousness of such knowledge comes the motivation to grow, to give one's best, to be "in pursuit of excellence." All such motivations help make not only the future more secure but also the present more fulfilling.

Pastor, your job is demanding, hard, nearly impossible. But as you respond to the challenges with dependence upon God's guidance and help, you will be equipped for meaningful ministry. Embrace each challenge as an opportunity—and see Him work!

# 12

# Survival Tactics

*So do not fear, for I am with you; do not be dismayed, for I
am your God. I will strengthen you and help you; I will
uphold you with my righteous right hand. All
who rage against you will surely be ashamed and disgraced;
those who oppose you will be as nothing and perish. . . . For
I am the LORD, your God, who takes hold of your right
hand and says to you, Do not fear; I will help you.*
—Isa. 41:10-11, 13

I LIKE THE TITLE OF STAN TOLER'S RECENT BOOK
*God Has Never Failed Me, but He's Sure Scared Me to Death a
Few Times.*[1] There is not a pastor living who cannot identify
with this thought. Ministry can be scary.

No one can give you a plan to eliminate the scary moments in ministry. There is no insulation against them, no
strategy that is foolproof, and no book that solves all the
problems. But God has given to each of us some inner resources that, if used properly, will strengthen our scary
moments and help us survive.

Consider the following survival tactics when you're
on the front lines:

*Pray.* God hears your prayers even when you are
scared, frustrated, confused, angry, and ready to quit. Because we live with a ministerial face most of the time, it is
sometimes hard for us to be transparent before God and
still believe He hears our prayers. But He sees and under-

stands the pain. Don't stop praying. "A people who can pray can never be overcome," Charles Spurgeon wrote, "because their reserve forces can never be exhausted."

*Be positive.* We've mentioned this previously. The hard, ugly moments of ministry can bring bitterness. The most helpful safeguard for the scary times is a positive attitude.

Viktor Frankl said, "The last of the human freedoms [is] to choose one's own attitude in any given set of circumstances, to choose one's way."[2] Frankl should know, for he survived a Nazi concentration camp ordeal by choosing the attitude of hope. A commitment to positive thoughts and responses may be the survival tactic you need.

*Encourage others.* When you encourage someone, you build the bridge to a better day. It is a law of life that in giving we become benefactors. When you lift another, you will be lifted. Norman Vincent Peale advised a person who was depressed and frustrated with life to find someone who needed him or her and to pour his or her life into that person's need. All of us have seen the results of an individual getting interested in another person's predicament, only to have his or her own attitude brighten. Encouragement may be the survival tactic you need.

*Read.* A good autobiography or biography is a helpful way to lift one's spirits. It is inspiring to understand the valleys through which others have walked and to see how the possibilities of God unfolded for them in the midst of dark days. Reading such books forces us to see that others have had trials worse than ours. That alone can take some of the sting from our hurt and bring hope to our situation.

Challenging books can help get our mind off our problem and invite us to think new thoughts, dream new dreams, and plan a new tomorrow. Reading can help us focus our mind on recovery, positive response, healing, and hope.

There are other ways to regroup. Take time for a hobby or a short overnight trip. Go shopping, browse through a bookstore, or visit an antique shop—something to help you refocus, clear the mind, settle the emotions. There are ways to survive a crisis, but you may have to work at finding the right way for you.

I read the tragic story of a boy whose body had been found following a kidnapping. The family was deeply grieved, as were his schoolmates. At the funeral a group of his school pals sang and, after their song, presented a banner to the parents. It read, "If his song is to continue, we must do the singing."[3] There is a message for pastors here. If the ministry to which God has called us is to continue after a crisis, a bad experience, a scary moment, we must be the ones to make it continue. If the song is to continue, we must do the singing!

# PREACHING MAKES A DIFFERENCE

# 13

# Someone Will Always Need Your Message

*Do not let your hearts be troubled. Trust in God;*
*trust also in me. In my Father's house are many rooms;*
*if it were not so, I would have told you. I am going*
*there to prepare a place for you. And if I go and*
*prepare a place for you, I will come back and take*
*you to be with me that you also may be where I am.*
—John 14:1-3

I RECALL SOMETHING THE LATE WILLIAM BARCLAY wrote to preachers: "Remember—there will always be someone present with a broken heart."

Some time ago when these words came back to me, they put me to thinking. Out of my thoughts came the reminder that every pastor will have someone listening to what God has given him or her to share. It is an encouraging thought indeed.

Too many times we let the voice of our critics or the apathy of some listeners dampen our motivation and preparation. But, pastor, there will always be someone who needs what you have to share!

Four types of people attend your church. The *first* are the type I have mentioned—the brokenhearted, hurting, lonely, and problem-laden people. They need you! They need what God wants to say to them—through you. You

are their link to good news and to hope. Let their needs—
and their support—be encouragement to you.

The *second* type of people who attend your church are
the good, faithful people. They are positive, optimistic,
supportive, and helpful. They love their pastor, pay their
tithes, pray for the church, serve, and reach out. They are
the "salt of the earth" people. They need you! They need
your love and encouragement to nurture all their positive
potential. They wait to hear what God will say to them
through your preaching and ministry. Let their support
and hunger encourage you.

A *third* type of people who attend your church are the
new families, the new Christians, people searching for answers to life's challenge and confusion. They need you!
They need a word from God. They need to be challenged
and directed by the gospel. Let their searching be an encouragement to your ministry. Be uplifted by their confidence.

A *fourth* group also attend your church—the critics,
power brokers, and negative thinkers. They also need your
ministry. They may not motivate you as much as the other
three groups, but God has a word for them—through you!
He has given them to you. Ministering to them, reaching
them, helping them will send you to your knees, and that
will make you a better pastor.

Pastor, take encouragement from the fact that three
out of four groups want to hear your message from God.
This should be enough to keep your head high and your
heart mellow and open. So, pastor, be encouraged!

# 14

# Preaching Is Significant

*When Jesus had called the Twelve together, he gave them*
*power and authority to drive out all demons and to cure*
*diseases, and he sent them out to preach the kingdom of*
*God and to heal the sick. He told them: "Take nothing for*
*the journey—no staff, no bag, no bread, no money, no extra*
*tunic. Whatever house you enter, stay there until you leave*
*that town. If people do not welcome you, shake the dust off*
*your feet when you leave their town, as a testimony against*
*them." So they set out and went from village to village,*
*preaching the gospel and healing people everywhere.*
—Luke 9:1-6

WILLIAM WILLIMON WROTE THAT "PEOPLE ARE RIPE
for a voice that gives them something significant worth living and dying for."[1] These are encouraging words. In an age
when some church growth specialists would tell us preaching is in decline, this is a strengthening thought.

Preaching is still a priority for pastors. Paul's admonition to Timothy, "Preach the Word" (2 Tim. 4:2), has not been
withdrawn, negotiated, or diminished. It is still a mandate.

Preaching is God's means of confronting people with
eternal truths. While it is not the only way, it has the promise of God's touch and His guidance. He reminds us concerning His Word, "It will not return to me empty, but will
accomplish what I desire and achieve the purpose for
which I sent it" (Isa. 55:11).

A few years ago I ran across these words from an installation prayer by Ed Towne: "O God, let me preach with enthusiasm because of what Christ did, not because of what the crowds think, . . . because of the salvation we have, not the size of the group we have. Use me, O God, not because it's the hour for the message, but because you've given me a message for the hour."[2]

The preaching event is a moment, if heart, mind, and spirit are prepared, when the eternal invades the present and life focuses on principles. Every pastor needs to know, as Willimon states, that "people are ripe for a voice that gives them something significant worth living and dying for." Pastor, know that what you preach will make a difference in someone's life—a significant difference in some. We are responsible to preach as best we can, with a heart and mind saturated with truth, prayed full with the Spirit of God, and eager to proclaim on God's behalf. The Holy Spirit will take such proclamations and plant them in the hearts and minds of hearers. This is a spiritual transaction preachers need to trust more than we do.

This is no time for casual preparation and passionless preaching. Herbert Carson wrote, "A preacher who has doubts about the gospel is a menace to any congregation. The pulpit is no place for hesitant uncertainty. It is a platform from which the herald of God announces with profound conviction the truth of God's own most holy Word."[3] Add to these thoughts the words of Craig Loscalzo: "Perhaps the downfall of preaching in the late twentieth century has been the proliferation of passionless preaching."[4]

The source for preaching and the cure for passionless preaching is, of course, the Word. We are not proclaimers of opinions nor dispensers of motivational talks—though a dynamic sermon will motivate. More, we are preachers of the Word—an eternal Word that gives substance and significance to our preaching. Dennis Kinlaw reminds us that "nothing in the world is as significant to a preacher as the day Scripture comes alive for him—the day when Scripture seizes him, when he knows that it belongs to him and he belongs to it."[5]

Preaching is still God's method of invading the human predicament with truth and hope. E. Stanley Jones reminded us that "congregations will gather around a pulpit from which living water is flowing."

There is a story from the French Revolution that tells of a group of political prisoners shut away in a dark, dingy dungeon. One of them had a Bible, and the other prisoners were eager to have him read it. But the darkness of the dungeon prohibited him from seeing the words. The only bit of light came from a tiny window near the ceiling, but for only a few minutes each day. The prisoners lifted their friend with the Bible onto their shoulders and into the sunlight. There, for a few minutes, he would read. Then they would lower him into their midst, and with anxious voices they would ask, "Tell us—what did you read while you were in the light?"[6] Our task as preachers is to stand before people and share what God has revealed to us "while [we] were in the light."

Pastor, God's mandate to us is to preach. His promise to us is that He will attend our preparation and anoint our preaching.

# 15

# Live by What You Preach

*Let the word of Christ dwell in you richly as you teach
and admonish one another with all wisdom, and as you
sing psalms, hymns and spiritual songs with gratitude
in your hearts to God. And whatever you do, whether in
word or deed, do it all in the name of the Lord Jesus,
giving thanks to God the Father through him.*
—Col. 3:16-17

THERE IS NOT A PASTOR ALIVE OR DEAD WHO HAS
not come up against the rough spots. They come with the
territory, the veterans will tell you. Life and pastoring during the hard times can be anything but fun. It can hurt.
Such moments can be long nights of the soul. Are there
any remedies?

The best remedies may be what you preach to your
people every Sunday. What you preach is evidently what
you believe. If it is good enough for your people, it is good
enough for you. What do you preach to your people? Probably something like this: "Just trust this situation to the
Lord." Or "Hang in there." Maybe it is "Have you prayed
about it?" Don't forget "God cares and will help you." We
have all used variations of these at one time or another.

Let's pursue a couple of these statements and see
what's in them for us when we hit rough spots.

*Just trust this situation to the Lord.* This seems too simple—but it is often a struggle. Often our troubles are

caused by things over which we have no control. Fretting and striving make no difference. Our best option is simply to give it to the Lord and entrust the solution to Him. This is not a cop-out, like the solution Jackie Gleason gave for the New York City traffic problem: "Make all the streets one way going north, and let Albany worry about the problem." When we give our problems to the Lord, we relinquish our dilemma and despair into His hands, trusting His care and His healing.

Another bit of preaching we do is summed up in the phrase *Hang in there.* This is encouragement for laypeople, and it is good advice for the preacher. There are times when the options are limited, and hanging in there is about all we can do. But it beats running, it's better than overreaction, and there are not a few who will tell you that's how they won the battle. They simple stayed the course, and a better tomorrow came. Pastor, God is with you in the "hang in there" moments.

The encouragement some people like to hear the most is *God cares and will help.* He does, and He will! One of my favorite verses is 1 Pet. 5:7 (PHILLIPS): "You can throw the whole weight of your anxieties upon him, for you are his personal concern." The caring God you commend to your people is also a God who cares for *you,* pastor.

Gladys Aylward, missionary to China a half century ago, was forced to leave her missionary work when the Japanese invaded Yangcheng. In fleeing certain death, she led nearly a hundred orphans over the mountains to Free China. It was a frightening journey. At times she was burdened by despair. One morning after a sleepless night, fearing they would never reach safety, she shared her hopelessness with the orphans. A 13-year-old girl reminded her of their much-loved story of Moses and the Israelites crossing the Red Sea.

"But I am not Moses," Gladys Aylward replied.

"Of course you aren't," the girl responded, "but Jehovah is still God!"[1]

Pastor, remember that God is still God. Let Him be large in your life, knowing that "you are [H]is personal concern." The God whom you commend to others wants to be God of your pains and suffering, your dark nights of the soul, and your despairing days. He wants to shepherd the one whom He has called.

# 16

# What Really Makes a Difference?

*If you obey my commands, you will remain in my love,*
*just as I have obeyed my Father's commands and*
*remain in his love. I have told you this so that my joy*
*may be in you and that your joy may be complete.*
—John 15:10-11

WHAT ARE THE THINGS THAT REALLY MAKE A DIF-
ference in our ministries? When the options are sifted out,
what remain as the rock-solid, dependable ingredients?
These are fair questions for the pastor, for there are times
when we are prone to wonder if anything works.

Fortunately, the things that make a real difference are
available to everyone. Of course, each of these come out of
a God-centered focus, which is one priority every pastor
will need. "It is only when ministry is truly God-centered,"
wrote Robert Callender, "that it becomes clearly focused
and we can see God's plan for us."[1]

Our God-centered life is what puts all the things that
matter into perspective. To use the resources of God without relationship with Him is to misuse God and to invite
disappointment.

*Prayer* is probably the most powerful tool for ministry
you have. It is an exercise of the soul that cannot be im-
proved upon. There will never be something to take its
place. It will never become obsolete. Prayer is one of your
greatest resources.

Charles Stanley, in his book *Handle with Prayer*, writes, "Many Christians are top-notch worriers and mediocre prayers."[2] Let's aspire to become top-notch persons of prayer. As we bare our souls to our Father through prayer, we have contact and communion with God. Max Lucado reminds us that Jesus responds, not to our eloquence, "but to our pain."[3]

There is a resource that will make a difference.

*The Word of God* is a second resource that will empower you for ministry. I have a devotional calendar that features this statement by Mountford: "For knowledge to become wisdom and for the soul to grow, the soul must be rooted in God." We are rooted in God as we spend time in the fertile soul of His Word. Scripture has a way of invading the heart and leading one out of darkness and into light.

In his book *Something Happens When Churches Pray*, Warren Wiersbe gives this counsel: "If your church is going through problems and difficulties, if Satan is opposing your work and using people in your community to make things difficult, what is the solution? The Word of God and prayer. That is the source of our wisdom, the success of our witness, the secret of our warfare."[4]

As pastors, we seek solutions, encouragement, a way through, and a way out. Pastor, you will find all of these in the Word of God. Among the last words of Pope Paul VI were these: "Apart from the Word of God, there are no valid solutions to the problems of our day."

A third resource that will help sustain you over the long haul is *obedience*. The word "obedience" is a much-maligned word. But God has not changed His mind about obedience. He has not renegotiated its terms or its importance. God still honors obedience. Sometimes in the low moments of ministry the only option may be simple obedience. But by our taking that step, God responds with blessing and with care.

John R. W. Stott, commenting on a phrase from Ps.

119:73, which reads, "Give me understanding, that I may learn thy commandments" (KJV), says "our whole nature fulfills its destiny only in obedience to the will of God."[5]

There are spiritual benefits to obedience—though that is not why we are obedient. Every pastor needs to know that God still honors the obedient heart. It is a rock-solid principle that really makes a difference. When ministry seems empty—maybe even hopeless—it is time to simply be obedient and trust the future to God. Such moments, while not easy, are a true test of your trust in the God who has called you. In the low moments of your soul, God has a way through for you, and you find it only along the path of obedience.

Pastor, the things that really matter are still intact. They are the handles for the soul through the narrow passageways. These resources never change. They will always be there, amid the everchanging environment and challenges. They are the things God has ordained, and He will honor those who use them.

# 17

# God Is in Action—Through You!

*In Damascus there was a disciple named Ananias.*
*The Lord called to him in a vision, "Ananias!" "Yes,*
*Lord," he answered. The Lord told him, "Go to the house*
*of Judas on Straight Street and ask for a man from Tarsus*
*named Saul, for he is praying. In a vision he has seen*
*a man named Ananias come and place his hands on him*
*to restore his sight." "Lord," Ananias answered, "I*
*have heard many reports about this man and all the*
*harm he has done to your saints in Jerusalem. And he*
*has come here with authority from the chief priests to*
*arrest all who call on your name." But the Lord said*
*to Ananias, "Go! This man is my chosen instrument to*
*carry my name before the Gentiles and their kings and*
*before the people of Israel. I will show him how much*
*he must suffer for my name." Then Ananias went to*
*the house and entered it. Placing his hands on Saul, he*
*said, "Brother Saul, the Lord—Jesus, who appeared to*
*you on the road as you were coming here—has sent me*
*so that you may see again and be filled with the Holy*
*Spirit." Immediately, something like scales fell from*
*Saul's eyes, and he could see again. He got up and*
*was baptized, and after taking some food, he regained*
*his strength. Saul spent several days with the disciples*
*in Damascus.*
—Acts 9:10-19

JAMES STEWART, IN HIS CLASSIC *HERALDS OF GOD*, wrote these encouraging words: "Every Sunday morning, when it comes, ought to find you awed and thrilled by this reflection. God is to be in action today through me for these people. This day may be crucial, this service decisive for someone now ripe for the vision of Jesus."[1]

What a great encouragement for any preacher! To realize we are in action every Sunday on behalf of God. The preacher in the biggest pulpit needs to hear this, as does the preacher in the smallest hamlet. It is a soul-stretching truth. It is a truth that will make every Sunday worth living and preparing for.

This is important to know, first, because each preacher needs to know the eternal reality of his or her call to preach. The preacher needs to know there is some purpose beyond the paycheck and some reason beyond the need for a job. There is a divine reality to the preaching event that overshadows all other ministerial events. It is the moment when one stands to declare the counsel of God.

There are days when a preacher needs to let this kind of reality invade the mind and heart, brushing back the bruises of pastoral life and lifting the spirits that have been dashed by careless words and petty conflicts. There will be times when one must pull away from the battle and let the heart be touched with the deep significance of preaching. For where one pulls aside, for a while, to hear the encouraging words of Stewart—and of God—he or she is encouraged to return to ministry with new vision and enthusiasm. To let the soul take in all that God designs by the preaching event is both refreshing and renewing.

This is important to know, also, because those who hear you preach need to know that God has a word for this situation. It was never safe to assume that those who heard us preach in past months or years had no problems and that life was flowing without any difficulty. It has never been that way. William Skudlarek has this to say about contemporary listeners/worshipers, as quoted in his book *The Word in Worship:*

> In the average parish congregation, about one fifth of the people will be feeling a sense of loss because of a recent bereavement. A third of them may be facing marital difficulties. About half of them will have problems of adjusting emotionally to school, job, home, or community. Others will be afflicted with a deep sense of guilt stemming from their inability to deal maturely with their sexuality, or because of their addiction to drugs or alcohol.[2]

When the preacher knows the hurts and heartaches of his or her listeners and also knows that he or she has a word from God, there is nothing more challenging and exciting. This is the task and the world of the preacher, who stands on Sunday with the one eternal Word that hurting people need to hear. He or she is "in action" for the God who can take the pieces of life and begin healing and ignite hope. To be part of such a dynamic possibility will help a preacher through some bad days, some awful board meetings, and some wrenching experiences. Pastor, be encouraged—reflect on the Sunday past and the Sunday coming. Remember: those days are crucial, for what you shared from God was decisive for someone. You were a link in a liberating moment; you were part of a beginning, a miracle, a new day!

This thought from Stewart, that "God is to be in action today through me for these people," is a truth that determines your significance far more than does a comment, a criticism, or a crisis. Too much of our self-esteem is determined by what others think of us. We let the comments, criticisms, and crises mold too much of our self-worth. And let's face it—they can be devastating, disheartening, and disastrous. They cannot be so easily put aside and forgotten. They sting. They hurt. They go deep. But, pastor, the good word from God that you share every Sunday is also a good word for *you!* One of those words may be crucial for you. There may be a word that will bring hope to your life and renewal to your spirit. For, you see, the God who ministers through you also ministers *to* you. It is a thought we need to write on the ledgers of our minds, to serve us in the times when we feel tested and weak.

The God who has called you to preach is the God who invites you to let yourself—your problems, your fears, your critics, your disappointments, your hurts—down into the grace of God and allow Him to nurture you, love you, and strengthen you.

Consider this great Old Testament verse, then a great New Testament word. The Old Testament word is from Isa. 30:18—"The LORD longs to be gracious to you; he rises to show you compassion. For the LORD is a God of justice. Blessed are all who wait for him!" The New Testament word is from Paul in Col. 2:10—"*You have everything when you have Christ,* and you are filled with God. . . . He is the highest Ruler, with authority over every other power" (TLB).

Pastor, the God of Isaiah and the God of Paul is your God! He changes not. His authority and power touch your ministry every time you are in action for Him. Let the strength of this thought be your encouragement for the day.

# LIFE IS A LEARNING EXPERIENCE

# 18

# So Much of Life Is Adjusting

*He who listens to a life-giving rebuke will be at home among the wise. He who ignores discipline despises himself, but whoever heeds correction gains understanding. The fear of the LORD teaches a man wisdom, and humility comes before honor.*
—Prov. 15:31-33

SOME TIME AGO MY DAUGHTER BOUGHT ME THE book *Beyond IBM*. A fascinating bit of information leaped out at me: "A rocket is on course only 2% of the time—the rest of the time it is correcting."[1]

It seems that ministry is like this—mostly correcting, adjusting. There are times when it seems that so little of ministry is "on course" and so much of it is "correcting."

I gave serious thought to what this bit of information might say to me. Let me share my reflections.

*First,* as a pastor I must praise God for the occasions when ministry is going well. One danger in ministry, as in all professions and jobs, is that the problems and bad moments have a way of obscuring the good times.

I believe God gives us the great moments of ministry, not only because they are fulfillments of His will and answers to the prayers of His people, but also to validate His goodness, authority, and power. As such, we should not forget them. God's caution to the children of Israel was that they would not forget the trips through the dry sea or the occasions when He provided for their needs.

*Second*, I must let the good times speak direction and assurance during the troubled times. The same God who blesses me with treasured experiences is the One who wants to guide, comfort, and protect me during the troubled moments. I need to remember this and draw strength from the God who is always there!

A few years ago I counseled a pastor whose ministry had crumbled due to poor judgment. He asked me the question every person asks at some time in his or her crisis: "Where is God?" I reminded the heartbroken pastor that God was where He always is—right here, available, comforting, loving, reaching out arms of understanding and forgiveness. He looked at me for a moment, as though the words formed a new truth. After a long pause he replied, "That's what we preach, isn't it?" He gave his defeat to God, and the road to recovery began.

*Third*, the troubled times are not totally lost. Sometimes out of the ashes comes beauty. Sometimes out of the chaos comes a deepened dependence upon God. Whatever is going on in crisis—pain or suffering, misunderstanding or confusion, separation or conflict—it forces us to adjust, correct, process, search, and stretch. While this process is painful and stress-laden, the possibility for resolution and growth is ever present.

Further, such dark moments provide opportunity for the light of His grace and glory to shine so beautifully to the heart. I asked a man not long ago what he had learned in what he called his "tunnel of agony." He replied, "That God's grace and help are more real than I ever thought."

What does all this have to do with adjusting and correcting? Just this: I must learn to adjust my circumstances to the grace and ways of God, rather than let my problems determine my view of God. I must be in a "correcting" mode so that life's situations let in the truths and promises of the gospel.

The more we live and pastor, the more we realize that life is on course such a brief time, and the rest of the time it is correcting.

# 19

# Lessons from a Rocket

*Therefore, dear friends, since you already know this, be on
your guard so that you may not be carried away by the
error of lawless men and fall from your secure position. But
grow in the grace and knowledge of our Lord and Savior
Jesus Christ. To him be glory both now and forever! Amen.*
—2 Pet. 3:17-18

LET'S THINK AGAIN ABOUT THE QUOTE FROM OUR
previous discussion—"A rocket is on course only 2% of the
time—the rest of the time it is correcting."[1] I like that bit of
statistic!

I was startled at first to realize that a rocket is on
course only 2 percent of the time! How does it ever reach
its destination? The answer is clear: the rest of the time it is
correcting.

All of us at times experience the less-than-perfect per-
formance, the missed opportunity, the good-intentioned
deed misinterpreted, or the blotched relationship. I am encouraged that rockets are not always on course and that
success is in correcting!

The correcting posture is what the pastor does best.
He or she is trained to respond, to adopt, to stretch, to pursue, to grow, to learn. The pastor prays and therefore seeks
guidance. So there should be no one who is more conscious that life is mostly correcting. Of all people, the pastor should be most conscious that he or she is less than

perfect. In fact, there are times one might think that being on course 2 percent of the time is a high estimate!

Where does all of this lead us? To three important conclusions. *First*, pastor, take heart—you don't have to be perfect! If you know how to do the correcting procedures, you will make it. It is not perfection your people seek. They want a pastor who is willing to serve, if not always perfectly. They want a pastor who will minister to needs, if not always in a perfect way.

*Second*, pastor, though you struggle at times, you can make the journey. You can bleed a little and still survive. You can mess it up, badly even, but still stay on the road. Why? Because life is more about correcting than about being perfect. The words "I'm sorry" and "I apologize" are great corrective lubricants that build relationships and put one back on the road to ministry and service. Joy comes from going the extra mile, offering forgiveness—and receiving forgiveness. It comes as we reach out to understand, rather than wait to be understood. It happens when we take another's hurt into our heart and offer healing. Out of the struggle, the pain, the humble journey of reconciliation, come strength and trust for the journey.

*Third*, pastor, out of the corrective times in ministry come some of the treasured memories of pastoral ministry. From an "I'm sorry" comes a new and better relationship. From an apology come a deeper trust and reconciliation. From a confession come healing and hope. From the struggle to forgive come peace and friendship.

So, pastor, learn from the rocket, which takes correcting as a part of the price to reach its destination. For you, it may be the price for effective, fulfilling ministry! May you have grace for the journey.

# 20

# A Lesson from the Prodigal Son's Father

*Jesus continued: "There was a man who had two sons. The younger one said to his father, 'Father, give me my share of the estate.' So he divided his property between them. Not long after that, the younger son got together all he had, set off for a distant country and there squandered his wealth in wild living. After he had spent everything, there was a severe famine in that whole country, and he began to be in need. So he went and hired himself out to a citizen of that country, who sent him to his fields to feed pigs. He longed to fill his stomach with the pods that the pigs were eating, but no one gave him anything. When he came to his senses, he said, 'How many of my father's hired men have food to spare, and here I am starving to death! I will set out and go back to my father and say to him: Father, I have sinned against heaven and against you. I am no longer worthy to be called your son; make me like one of your hired men.' So he got up and went to his father. But while he was still a long way off, his father saw him and was filled with compassion for him; he ran to his son, threw his arms around him and kissed him. The son said to him, 'Father, I have sinned against heaven and against you. I am no longer worthy to be called your son.' But the father said to his servants, 'Quick! Bring the best robe and put it on him.*

*Put a ring on his finger and sandals on his feet. Bring the*
*fattened calf and kill it. Let's have a feast and celebrate. For*
*this son of mine was dead and is alive again; he was lost*
*and is found.' So they began to celebrate."*
—Luke 15:11-24

HAVE YOU EVER CONSIDERED THE LOVING FATHER
in the story commonly called the parable of the prodigal
son? How long had this brokenhearted father waited?
Surely he spent a lot of time in prayer. Did he grow weary
in petitioning God? Did he share his sorrows with his
friends or his other son?

As I consider that father who cared so deeply, I wonder if nearly every pastor can identify with him. Sometimes when you have cared the most, spent long hours,
and tried everything, church members up and leave,
thirsty for something better. And though the father cared,
he was rejected, left standing and waiting—still caring.

Pastor, there will be times when love and care will be
rejected, taken advantage of, turned upon and misunder-
stood, misused and abused. These times should not turn
your love to hate nor your caring to indifference.

There are several things the loving father did from
which you can draw encouragement:

1. He continued to care, to wait, and to love, knowing
it would be worth it all when the son came home. Most
prodigals will come home. Some never do. But to have
love and care ready for the homecoming of some son or
daughter is what gives joy to ministry and strength to
serving.

Many people will pass through your lives during the
years of your ministry. Some will find help, be strength-
ened for their journey, and carve out a place in their hearts
for you forever. Others will leave for a thousand reasons;
some will be valid, and some will not. Nurture love and
care in your heart regardless of what the prodigals do up-

on leaving. Their words may be sharp, their criticisms harsh, and their exodus cruel and demeaning. Don't let the pain taint your heart or steal your love. For some other day, in some other place, you may welcome a prodigal, unknown to you, who is away from home. You will need the Father's love and a caring heart.

2. The father made himself available to others. Because the father loved, waited, and cared, any prodigal coming down the road could learn some new lessons from him. Every pastor has welcomed people into his or her fellowship only to learn they came from "somewhere else." They left another church, walked out on another pastor, and are now on a journey. Who cannot help but think, "Will it happen to me?" The father wraps his arms around the people from "somewhere else" and pours himself into their lives. And because love and care have special ways of changing, nurturing, uplifting, and building, the people from "somewhere else" are blessed, accepted, loved, and given the atmosphere in which to grow, to learn, and to be different.

3. The father did not spend his time nursing his wounds. Did he hurt? Yes! Was the rejection painful? Certainly. Did he hate to see his son go? By all means. But the father moved forward despite the pain, determining to keep love alive. Pastor, establish ahead of time that the deep hurts from ministry will not blow out the candle of love in your heart.

So, pastor, be encouraged! Some will go and never return. Others will come into your ministry, needing your love and care. Keep it alive for those prodigals who desperately need it! And the joy of loving will heal the hurts of rejection.

# 21

# Another Look at Success

*God is not unjust; he will not forget your work*
*and the love you have shown him as you have helped*
*his people and continue to help them. We want each*
*of you to show this same diligence to the very end,*
*in order to make your hope sure.*
—Heb. 6:10-11

EVERYONE IS INTERESTED IN SUCCESS. WE ARE
hooked on the idea. We expend a great deal of effort and
time to experience it. The desire to succeed is not bad, for if
it is channeled in the right direction, much can be accom-
plished for the glory of God.

But let's face it—the thought of success is a bittersweet
encounter for some pastors. They have given their all in effort and energy. They have sacrificed, strained, and stud-
ied, only to see success elude their efforts. Such pastors are
left to ponder one of the great inequities of life.

Too often pastors count the years and the work, total
the sacrifices and the faithfulness, compare it to a success
model, and are overwhelmed by the futility of the para-
dox. At such times the enemy whispers despairing
thoughts that intrude and intimidate.

Is there a good word for a pastor like that? One comes
from our Lord, who said,

> And why do you worry about clothes? See how the
> lilies of the field grow. They do not labor or spin. Yet I tell

you that not even Solomon in all his splendor was dressed like one of these. If that is how God clothes the grass of the field, which is here today and tomorrow is thrown into the fire, will he not much more clothe you, O you of little faith? So do not worry, saying, "What shall we eat?" or "What shall we drink?" or "What shall we wear?" For the pagans run after all these things, and your heavenly Father knows that you need them. But seek first his kingdom and his righteousness, and all these things will be given to you as well *(Matt. 6:28-33)*.

Another comes from the late Dag Hammarskjöld, who wrote, "Never let success hide its emptiness from you, achievement its nothingness, toil its desolation. And so . . . keep alive the incentive to push on further, that pain in the soul which drives us beyond ourselves. . . . Do not look back."[1]

When we look squarely at our concept of success and force it to yield to reality, we silence its urging to compare ourselves with another. Such an exercise will bring us to proper priority for our lives. We can then feel the surge of purpose and the adrenaline of hope.

Edward Dayton wrote that "to succeed is to have a sense of self-satisfaction, a feeling of rightness about what one has done and is doing, along with the results of doing it."[2]

Our pursuit, then, is not success. Our pursuit is mission—our reason for living. When we can get a clear picture of who we are, what we are about—and whose we are—then we are ready for the future. Success, then, comes on our terms rather than those prescribed by our peers and leaders or by some other measurement. When we get a grip on our mission, we set life in the direction to accomplish that mission, undeterred by success stories.

Where life takes this kind of initiative, it marches to a different drummer and walks to a new order. In his book *Serving God*, Ben Patterson quotes Ruben Alves's defining of hope as "hearing the melody of the future."[3] Throughout the stuff of life, the pastor needs to hear the summons of God on his or her life. With renewed vision and vigor, we can go onward in mission, "hearing the melody of the future."

Pastor, success is not the measuring stick with God; faithfulness is. The good word is that you can—and should—be faithful. In faithfulness comes fulfillment and peace, which in the deepest sense constitute success.

# 22

# How to Deal with Pressure

*Therefore, I urge you, brothers, in view of God's mercy,*
*to offer your bodies as living sacrifices, holy and pleasing*
*to God—this is your spiritual act of worship. Do not*
*conform any longer to the pattern of this world, but be*
*transformed by the renewing of your mind. Then you*
*will be able to test and approve what God's will is—*
*his good, pleasing and perfect will.*
—Rom. 12:1-2

WE COULD PROBABLY ALL AGREE ON THE FACT THAT
there are lots of pressures in pastoral ministry. It hardly draws
a breath of debate. Our task as pastors is not to fear the pressures, but to deal with them in a positive way.

Hudson Taylor wrote, "It doesn't matter how great the
pressure is. What really matters is *where the pressure lies—*
whether it comes between you and God or whether it
presses you nearer His heart."

Are you experiencing pressure? Is it self-imposed?
Sometimes we are our own worst enemies, setting expectations that are unrealistic, unwise, or ill timed. These create
unneeded pressure and the certain outcome of disappointment, frustration, and defeat. Too often such pressures
drive capable persons from the pastorate.

So how do we deal with these internal pressures? Be
realistic in your dreams, plans, and ambitions. The drive
for success and accomplishment is good only to a point.

One needs to know how to balance all the dreams and plans with ministry, family, health—all of life. When any part is out of balance, undue stress will result.

Pastor, I believe we can lay our dreams, plans, and ambitions before God and seek His wisdom. When we have His counsel, better and wiser expectations begin to form. We *can* set our expectations and chart our future in ways that create balance rather than pressure.

How do we deal with external stressors—pressures from others, from family, from leaders, and so on? A large part of our pressure comes from people imposing expectations on us—often unrealistic, but nonetheless demanding.

There are no easy solutions. Consider the following possibilities:

1. Seek God. He is where we always begin when dealing with pressure problems. Pastor, He who called you is more interested in your battles than you are. "The one who is in you is greater than the one who is in the world" (1 John 4:4).

2. Talk with others. How have they handled similar situations? Seek the counsel of trusted friends and colleagues. Observe how those you respect handle pressure.

3. Read and research. Find out what is available as a resource. Often good articles, books, or seminars can open a window on a pressure point that not only is a solution to your problem but also provides a wider learning experience.

4. Learn to say no. It is an option! We are not all things to all people. Sometimes God's call and priority for our lives is a great deal different from the expectations of our friends, members, or even family. Learn to say no graciously.

5. Prioritize. At some point, we have to decide what the priorities are for our lives, then protect those priorities by either delegating lesser expectations or simply leaving them undone.

6. Examine the source of the pressure. Maybe a faith-

ful member, a friend, or a family member is right in creating pressure in your life. Don't assume that all pressure is bad. Maybe God is getting your attention through others, and through them He may be saying some needed and worthwhile things. Learn to be objective, sensitive to the who and what of the pressure.

Hudson Taylor's advice was good—see to it that the pressure "presses you nearer His heart." For there, under His care and His guidance, there is a way through.

# YOU ARE GOD'S RESPONSIBILITY

# 23

# God Has the Last Word

*"Though the mountains be shaken and the hills be*
*removed, yet my unfailing love for you will not be*
*shaken nor my covenant of peace be removed," says*
*the* LORD, *who has compassion on you.*
—Isa. 54:10

I HAD THE PRIVILEGE A FEW MONTHS AGO OF AT-
tending homecoming at my alma mater, Olivet Nazarene
University, in Kankakee, Illinois. A number of people and
events there encouraged me.

I met an old college/seminary friend who had years
ago gone through a crushing experience in his marriage.
His ministry was ripped from him. It was the lowest moment of his life. His future was blurred, uninviting, and
scary.

Then God began putting the pieces of a ministry together for my friend. Today he serves as pastor of one of
the fastest-growing churches in America. From failure to
fantastic! As I talked with him, I mentioned how beautiful
it was to see how God had shepherded him through the
dark hours and had given him such a great ministry. He
gave God all the credit. It was encouraging to know that
failure doesn't have to be the last word!

I was encouraged to realize again that God brings victory from tragedy. The university had recently witnessed
the tragic deaths of three of its students in a van accident.

The Orpheus Choir was en route to Indianapolis to partici-
pate in the Gaither Praise Gathering when the van, with 11
choir members, overturned, killing 3 of its passengers. The
tragedy left the campus numb, overwhelmed, and griev-
ing.

But God was at work in the midst of sorrow. I saw the
comforting presence of Christ bring the students together
and bond them in their moment of sorrow and grief. The
coronation ceremony became a moving witness to the
power of grace and Christian healing. One of the victims of
the crash had been elected to the queen's court. Her Christian testimony made a profound impact. The tragedy, all of
a sudden, had put the value of life and death in Christian
perspective.

And though Olivet lost its homecoming football game
that day, I was reminded that the team has regrouped and
will play again. The coach will take the team back to the
drawing board; they will review their defeat, but only with
the purpose of winning the next game. Defeat is not the
end of the journey.

Failure, tragedy, and defeat are never the last words
for the Christian. They are occasions for God to speak to
us, to nurture us, to comfort and guide us, to write the
chapters of hope that put life back to its task.

Pastor, perhaps you are going through a low moment,
a down time, a tragedy, a defeat, a crushing experience. Do
not let these be the final chapters in a ministry of a life. At
a low moment in his life, Wesley wrote, "I consulted God
in His Word." God has a word for you, and it is a word of
hope, about going forward, about picking up the pieces,
and about resting in the grace of God.

# 24

# How Does a Pastor Handle Failure?

*But you, O Israel, my servant, Jacob, whom I have chosen, you descendants of Abraham my friend, I took you from the ends of the earth, from its farthest corners I called you. I said, "You are my servant"; I have chosen you and have not rejected you.*
*—Isa. 41:8-9*

THE GREATEST EFFORTS, THE MOST DEDICATED ATtempts sometimes wind up as failure. Alex MacKenzie wrote a book, *Time for Success*, in which he said "success is doing your best."[1] Too few will settle for this. In Christian service the only failure is failure to do the will of God. That is a truth all of us need to hear repeatedly and to appropriate for ourselves and others.

Sometimes the success syndrome becomes so demanding that it's almost bigger than life. It towers over us like a giant, speaking all the ugly thoughts that shatter and destroy our self-image. And yet God calls us to present our successes and our failures to Him. Our failure, given to God, can be raw material with which He charts another path and opens another door. All He desires is our relinquishment of the failure and our willingness to go forward in obedience to His next chapter for life. Denis Haack has reminded us that "the Lord has promised to return soon.

Until then, we are to be faithful. That means faithfulness with wealth, fame, power, self-fulfillment, and appearance—or without them."[2]

Success is easy to handle. When things are going well, faithfulness seems easy to identify and implement. But failure brings an environment of guilt, self-doubt, and resentment. We can begin to believe we cannot receive God's care and help, especially if sin and disobedience caused us to fail.

Pastor, you must do the hard task of stewardship when failure comes. You must pick up the pieces, give them to God, and see what His next marching orders are for life. You need to know that failure does not keep us from His grace and compassion.

Shelley Chapin's life was arrested early by cancer. Her dreams and successes faded. "Failure" seemed the only appropriate word to summarize her journey. But Shelley fought back, using what life had dealt to her for the glory of God. Toward the end of her ordeal she wrote, "I was to learn that all of life depends on grace. Each breath I take, every song I sing, every prayer I offer, and every plan I make—all grow out of grace. . . . Learning to see our lives as a gift, one day at a time, is an important part of living in this world."[3]

One way a pastor handles failure is to shift the focus from success to service. If what we had offered to God comes to failure, He is partner with us in the failure. He will not leave us there to drown in self-pity and remorse. He will not abandon us along the road of faithfulness.

Renewing our vision for success in the light of failure brings fresh caution. It forces us to examine our efforts, our disciplines, and our accountability. Not every failure is our fault. Nor is every failure the fault of another. Somewhere there needs to be a place where we process all of it with God and ready ourselves for the journey onward.

Toward the end of his life, Albert Einstein removed from his wall the portraits of two scientists—Newton and

Maxwell. He replaced them with portraits of Gandhi and Schweitzer. He explained it was time to replace the image of success with the image of service.

The pastor keeps before himself or herself the image of service to Christ and His kingdom. The image of service places a proper view on success, but more important, it gives interpretation and comfort to failure.

# 25

# Our Help Comes from the Lord

*I lift up my eyes to the hills—where does my help come from? My help comes from the LORD, the Maker of heaven and earth. He will not let your foot slip—he who watches over you will not slumber; indeed, he who watches over Israel will neither slumber nor sleep. The LORD watches over you—the LORD is your shade at your right hand; the sun will not harm you by day, nor the moon by night. The LORD will keep you from all harm— he will watch over your life; the LORD will watch over your coming and going both now and forevermore.*
—Ps. 121

AT THE END OF EACH YEAR I TRY TO READ A COUPle of books I had read in previous years and which meant a great deal to me. This past year I pulled Gerald Kennedy's book *Fresh Every Morning* from the shelf and reread again the words of the great Methodist bishop. A particular passage stood out to me; I noticed that the other times I had read this book I had not marked it for any reason. Among other things, it is a reminder that the years and circumstances bring different needs into our lives. The passage that caught my attention reads, "It is amazing how many of the troubles which loom so large as we look far ahead never materialize. God is always visiting us with divine surprises and miraculously eliminating some of the obstacles in our way. If I can finish the day, tomorrow will have some fresh light which will illuminate the dark picture."[1]

*"How many of the troubles which loom so large as we look far ahead never materialize."* It would probably do all of us good to keep track of our anticipated troubles for a while, if for nothing else but to see how few of them ever happen. And even when they do, the pastor can take comfort from the fact that God is in the midst of the worst, trying to bring something good out of each situation.

A little girl asked her father what God was doing during a severe thunderstorm. She answered her own question after a second's thought by saying, "Oh, I know—He's making the morning."

Pastor, God is in the midst of your worst troubles, creating morning and light, putting together a new day, a way out. He is the Architect of victory, not defeat. Kennedy put it like this: *"If I can finish the day, tomorrow will have some fresh light which will illuminate the dark picture."* And thank God it is so!

If troubles do come, and surely some will, God is God of the darkness and the troubled times, as well as the Master of light and victory. We sometimes feel that God is there just when the victory is unfolding, when the morning comes, when there is something to write home about. But the reason there is victory is because He has been at work in the defeated moments of our life. The reason there is light and rejoicing is because He was at work in the darkness. When the lights go out in our world, in our careers, in our assignments, and when it seems there is no way out, no tomorrow, no hope—God feels what we feel. He will wrestle with the worst to bring us to victory. Pastor, be encouraged: "In all these things we are more than conquerors through him who loved us" (Rom. 8:37).

Another statement in Gerald Kennedy's book encourages me as well: "The preacher ought to recognize that his job is to tell people where their help is."[2] Pastor, remind yourself on occasion where your help is. Frequently you will be prescribing your own cure as you proclaim hope and healing to your people.

In his book *What's a Nice God like You Doing in a Place like This?* Wesley Tracy tells of Earl Wolf's sister, who fought a long battle with cancer. Dr. Wolf made the trip from Missouri to Pennsylvania to attend her funeral. While he was there, he spent some time leafing through his sister's Bible. He found this handwritten poem tucked in its pages:

> *Often on the Rock I tremble,*
> *Faint of heart and weak of knee;*
> *But the steadfast Rock of Ages*
> *Never trembles under me.*[3]

So, pastor, draw strength from the Lord in your troubled times, assured that He is working on your behalf. And be comforted with the fact that whatever He is doing, it is good, and it will be right.

# 26

# Draw Strength from Your Call to Preach

*Yet when I preach the gospel, I cannot boast, for I am compelled to preach. Woe to me if I do not preach the gospel! If I preach voluntarily, I have a reward; if not voluntarily, I am simply discharging the trust committed to me. What then is my reward? Just this: that in preaching the gospel I may offer it free of charge, and so not make use of my rights in preaching it.*
—1 Cor. 9:16-18

"IF ANYTHING CAN HAPPEN, IT CAN HAPPEN TO A pastor," said one pastor after a hectic week. Who could argue with his conclusion? The pastor is at the center of life's agony and action. If there is a crisis, a death, an accident—which are only a few possibilities—the pastor gets involved. All such activities, added to the regular agenda of the pastorate, add stress, time pressures, frustration, and physical weariness.

In such times, pastors can draw strength from God's presence and from the confirmation and assurance of their call to preach. While the call to preach has been debated and kicked around a little, it has not lost its validity. Make sure of yours before stepping into the pastorate. More than one pastor will tell you that it was their call to preach that kept them going and surviving the hard times.

One's call to preach is a sacred and inspiring trust. With the assurance of a call ringing in the heart and soul, a pastor can survive about any crisis and endure the deepest disappointment. I heard a pastor say some years ago that the call to preach wasn't nearly as important as it once was. That's news to me. In fact, while I don't think it ever becomes more or less important in one era as opposed to another, I do believe that especially for these times and for these pressures a pastor had better make sure of his or her calling.

Consider the call to preach:

1. When God calls, He forms a partnership with that individual, to strengthen, equip, and guide. It is a truth from which we need to draw, perhaps more than we do. Ever and again we need to return to our call and be encouraged by its reality. As one gathers strength from his or her call to preach, motivation and inspiration—and even strength—come for ministry.

2. Plant your crises, your discouragements, your frustrations in your call to preach. Let your call be the reference point to which you return, again and again, to gain perspective for all that is happening. The temptation is in the low times to see other options and pursue other jobs. Do not let the hard times force you to regretful decision making.

Occasionally God does direct someone to leave pastoral ministry. He may release a pastor to pursue other occupations or other forms of ministry. But for most pastors this does not happen. Instead, it's very important to keep the perspective of his or her call when the pressures are on and the going gets rough.

So do not doubt your call to preach in the midst of your deepest crisis, when the emotions are being assaulted and all the arrows are pointing downward. Such moments are not the best for clear thinking and decision making. Rest in those moments on your call, and let its strength bring healing for recovery and renewal.

3. Even when one has the assurance of a call to preach, that is not enough. One must stay spiritually fit. The call must be nurtured and given a heart where it can grow and accomplish its purpose. Prayer and study of the Word must be priorities for the person with a call to preach. One may have all the gifts available and the advantages of education, but without channeling these in a heart warmed at the altar of God, they will fail. Usually one's spiritual life will determine how well he or she survives the rough terrain of pastoral ministry.

4. One's call to preach must be fulfilled in a body that is fit and a mind that is equipped. Physical fitness is important in pastoral ministry. Exercise should be a priority. Much stress builds simply because the physical has not been attended to. Also, the mind must be exercised. If one is focused only on problems, crises, buildings, finances, and so on, the romance of ministry soon fades. A deterrent to such possibilities is to study, read, and fill the mind with thoughts that lift one above the battles. A good organizational system will also help relieve one from the haunting question "What am I forgetting?" Attention to these items will help one fulfill his or her calling in a better way.

Pastor, the God who called you wants to be Partner with you in ministry.

# 27

# The Barren Times

*The desert and the parched land will be glad; the
wilderness will rejoice and blossom. Like the crocus, it
will burst into bloom; it will rejoice greatly and shout for
joy. The glory of Lebanon will be given to it, the splendor
of Carmel and Sharon; they will see the glory of the* LORD,
*the splendor of our God. Strengthen the feeble hands,
steady the knees that give way; say to those with fearful
hearts, "Be strong, do not fear; your God will come, he
will come with vengeance; with divine retribution he will
come to save you." Then will the eyes of the blind be
opened and the ears of the deaf unstopped.*
—Isa. 35:1-5

THERE ARE TIMES, IF WE ARE HONEST, WHEN THE
very work of ministry seems dry and barren. In such times
the soul asks the whys and may be tortured by doubts.
There has never been a pastor exempt from such occasions.
The biographies of great pastors include their dark moments of the soul.

For some, admitting to the dryness is the admission of
failure. The very thought weighs so heavily it almost short-
circuits any possibility for recovery. But dryness is not nec-
essarily failure. Take courage, face the facts, put your emotions in context, then move on, with faith that God will
help you write a new chapter of ministry. He will—with
your help! The words of Jeremy Taylor are helpful: "It is

impossible for that man to despair who remembers that his Helper is omnipotent."

For others, admitting to dryness gives occasion to the "victim" syndrome. One begins playing the "if only" game. The blame game creates a no-win situation. Rather than facing the facts, it focuses on others. It invites self-pity. It only paralyzes the person who needs to seek help and sketch a new day. In *If Only*, David A. Seamands writes about "the obsession with victimism or victimology. This is the Great Blame Game in which people try to escape personal responsibility for their choices and excuse almost any kind of behavior by finding somebody else to blame."[1]

Others see admitting the dryness as ego damaging. Their arrogance blinds them to such a problem. "It could never happen to me," they say. While they are quick to see it in others, they never see it in themselves. Calvin Miller has written of a time in his ministry when such was his problem:

> I cried out to God to slay me or make me an honest man with an authentic word. My intellectual pride dissolved in utter need. I broke! My brokenness—like all brokenness—had for its sweet fruit, simple fluent tears. Those tears were sheer acetylene. A torch that cut away, at first, my pride, and then my doubt. With arrogance and doubt both gone, the scales fell from my eyes. I saw God! High and lifted up![2]

For some the dry and barren times come because to some degree they invite them. Sometimes one loses focus and passion for ministry by digressing to other things. In his book *Margin*, Richard A. Swenson quotes Christopher Lasch, who talks about our "baffled sense of drift."[3] If a pastor does not keep his or her heart and mind focused on God, it is easy to be drawn away by other things. Too much attention to other things can create dryness in the soul and barrenness in ministry. The cure for such dryness is to give priority to the spiritual. It is to give attention to one's call and to be steward of the responsibilities God has placed in your care. This may well be one of the biggest problems with contemporary ministry—loss of focus because of too many interests outside the ministry.

Some see dryness as an end to ministry, God's withdrawal of blessing, His signal to bring closure to ministry. But is it really? Could it not be a time to do spiritual evaluation and inventory? Could it not be a time to renew passion for ministry and people? To recapture the joy of service and preaching? Pastor, be encouraged—in the dry times there is opportunity to meet God and have the heart touched again with the fire and purging of His love. The God who called you to preach is the One waiting to touch the dryness with life, with fire, and with passion. In *The Life God Blesses*, Gordon MacDonald talks about "developing the muscles of the soul." He writes, "The life God blesses is a life lived out of the soul—that place where God meets a person."[4]

Pastor, the dry times can be times of growth, learning, and submission. Our response and reactions will determine how we survive, how we rebound. They will determine the future of our ministries. Someone has written, "In the presence of trouble some people grow wings; others buy crutches."

Stay close to God in the dry times. Seek His face. Study His Word. Let the spiritual resources bathe your soul until the dryness gives way to tears and recovery. Your faith in God's faithfulness is crucial. He will touch the waiting heart with newness, with vision, and with hope.

# 28

# Thank God for the Joy of Ministry

*Rejoice in the Lord always. I will say it again: Rejoice!*
—Phil. 4:4

THERE IS JOY IN MINISTRY! THIS MUST BE A PREMISE on which we build ministry, or the New Testament is suspect. The gospel, which is the central priority of ministry, means "good news." If we are dispensers of good news, then joy is a by-product of the proclamation.

Amid all the negatives that come with ministry, we must not lose sight of the joy, the victory, and the fulfillment that should also define it. In a negative world it is too easy to color ministry with the wrong hues.

Paul's word to the Philippian church was "Rejoice in the Lord always. I will say it again: Rejoice!" We must have a place in ministry for rejoicing, for joy, for victory—a place to savor the success of faithful ministry.

*One* way to thank God for the joy of ministry is to acknowledge His blessings. Let's not see storm clouds in every success. We must boldly express our thanks for the victories and live those moments with gratitude and joy.

*Another* way to thank God for the joy of ministry is to live with a spirit of expectancy. As I visit with those who are experiencing the joys of ministry, I am encouraged by them. They not only see, feel, and appreciate the blessings of ministry but also are anticipating more of them. They see potential, they dream of better things, and they are not waiting for the next crisis. There is a spirit of expectancy in their ministry. It is contagious. It not only infuses their soul with joy but also spreads to their congregations. Joy and expectancy come alive in the Body of Christ.

A *third* way to thank God for the joy of ministry is to keep the focus on Christ. Those who celebrate the joy of ministry keep close to the One who called them. They celebrate relationship. They know the Source of joy and saturate life with His presence and with His will. They have a sense of dependence, which creates authentic ministry. Theirs is a ministry for God, not a ministry for self. Out of such a relationship comes joy, fulfillment, and a sense of usefulness. One can truly celebrate success when the focus is on Christ. For them, every victory is genuine, and every battle is for a great cause.

Yet *another* way to thank God for the joy of ministry is to keep exploring the potential. Successful pastors keep their energies engaged in the big picture. They give themselves to eternal causes. They accept problems as part of the journey, but not the whole journey. They give themselves to what Stephen Covey calls, "First things first." Where life is focused on potential more than on problems, there the Spirit unleashes energies and gifts "for the work of the ministry" (Eph. 4:12, KJV). Such focus is the raw material for joy.

*One other* observation of those who thank God for the joy of ministry: they seek to serve and not to be served. Someone has written that "fragrance always clings to the hand that gives roses." Successful pastors reap the benefits of servanthood.

Warren Wiersbe, in his book *On Being a Servant of God*, wrote, "If the worker doesn't get a blessing out of the work, something is radically wrong. Serving God isn't punishment; it is nourishment. Jesus said, 'My food is to do the will of him who sent me and to finish his work' (John 4:34)."[1] Wise pastors enjoy serving.

These are some ways to thank God for the joy of ministry. For where there is no thanks, there is no joy. All the victories of ministry are the by-product of faithfulness, and one of the tasks of faithfulness is thanksgiving. Years ago I heard E. Stanley Jones say he spent his mornings thanking and praising God, honoring and deepening his relationship with Him. It was the secret to his life of joy.

"Let God be large in your life this week," I heard a Sunday School teacher say one Sunday. Thanksgiving is letting God be large in our hearts. In ministry many things clamor for our attention. Stay up-to-date with your "thank-Yous," for I am convinced that thankfulness is a deterrent to selfishness. It is a reminder that your life and ministry are dependent on others and especially on God. Thanksgiving turns your thoughts to God, to His blessings, to His plans, and to His counsel. All of these prepare you for success, for joy, and for exciting ministry.

# 29

# The Romance of Ministry

*I thank Christ Jesus our Lord, who has given me strength,
that he considered me faithful, appointing me to his
service. Even though I was once a blasphemer and a
persecutor and a violent man, I was shown mercy because
I acted in ignorance and unbelief. The grace of our
Lord was poured out on me abundantly, along with
the faith and love that are in Christ Jesus.*
—1 Tim. 1:12-14

THERE IS ROMANCE IN MINISTRY. SOME WILL DOUBT the very words. But there is romance in ministry—for we are in partnership with God. Ministry is God's business, not ours. For too many the ministry is a solo journey. And without God as our Partner, ministry loses its romance and its motivation. Paul wrote to Timothy, "I thank Christ Jesus our Lord, who has given me strength, that he considered me faithful, appointing me to his service." He reminds us in Philippians of our "partnership in the gospel" (1:5).

There is romance in ministry—for we are in the greatest partnership in the world. It is a humbling thought to realize that God has called us to be His spokespersons with so great a message. When we comprehend all that means, we can only be encouraged that we are in partnership with the God of the universe, the Source of all our abilities, the Fountain of all our strength, and the Wellspring of all our words. There is romance in such a partnership.

There is romance in ministry—for we are in a grand relationship. Heidi Husted, in an article titled "Four Ways I've Found Encouragement," tells of a relationship with a spiritual mentor and how this mentor "helped me listen to my life. She has been a reminder that there is a huge difference between working for God and being with God," Husted wrote.[1] Our partnership with God is not just "doing ministry." It is a relationship of redemption—He is our Savior. It is a relationship of love—He loves us, not because we do ministry, but for who we are. It is a relationship of covenant—He is committed to us beyond our comprehension. He is Father to us. He is Comforter. He is Healer. He is our "all in all" (1 Cor. 15:28; cf. Col. 3:11). Relationship entails relating. God related himself to us by bringing His love, His Spirit, His resources, and spreading them on the table of our souls. In this relationship He invites us to partake at His table, to be nourished, to be fed, to be equipped for ministry. There is romance in such a relationship!

There is romance in ministry—for we have a great cause. Kevin A. Miller, editor of *Leadership*, tells of being at a conference where people were asked to pray for one another in the closing session. During that prayer, Miller said, one woman prayed this prayer for him: "Thank you, Lord, that you have entrusted him with the gospel of Christ."[2] There is romance in a cause, a mission bigger than life. The ministry is a trust. God entrusts those whom He calls with the most thrilling news the world has ever heard.

There is romance in ministry—for we are servants. Servanthood is a strange concept to the materialistic world. It is contrary to the mind-set that considers only "what's in it for me." God calls us to a cross, to sacrifice, and to service. These are uncomfortable terms to the secular mind. But for the Christian they are the terms of life; they are the rites of passage for the spiritual journey. Paul wrote often about his being a "servant of Christ Jesus." Jesus gave us one of His kingdom principles when He said, "Whoever wants to become great among you must be your servant, and whoever wants to be first must be slave of all" (Mark 10:43-44). Jesus knew something about human nature. True fulfillment comes from serving, not being served.

There is romance in ministry—for we are touching the lives of people. We can view people in two ways—as problems or as potential. No one would deny there are problem people in our world. And they get a lot of press! If we are not careful, we could conclude that all people are problems. Romance in the ministry comes from helping people, sharing God's good Word with them, seeing it take root in their lives, and rejoicing as they bear fruit. Romance comes from touching the lives of people in their moment of crisis and sensing their warm, affirming response. You know, then, that you are an ambassador of God. Romance comes from comforting people in their hour of despair and knowing you make a difference. Romance comes from sharing the joys of people, knowing you are an important part of their lives. In their book *Pastors at Risk,* H. B. London Jr. and Neil B. Wiseman wrote, "Who else has a commission from God to walk into the main events of the human drama as a proxy for the Living Christ?"[3] There is romance in helping people.

Pastor, there is romance in ministry! This is not to say that every day is a celebration of success. But the victories of ministry build a legacy of joy that sustains us through the years.

# 30

# Enjoy Your Successes!

*"For I know the plans I have for you," declares the LORD,*
*"plans to prosper you and not to harm you, plans to give*
*you hope and a future. Then you will call upon me and*
*come and pray to me, and I will listen to you. You will seek*
*me and find me when you seek me with all your heart."*
—Jer. 29:11-13

WHAT DO YOU DO WITH SUCCESS? ENJOY IT! THANK God for it! Celebrate! Rejoice! Count your blessings! Savor the moment! Remember it—for a long time!

Over the years your ministry will experience grand moments of accomplishment. The pastorate can be the greatest profession in the world. Maybe not all the time, for success is not an all-the-time thing in any area of life. But in the ministry we need to believe that victory and fulfillment can characterize our career.

To begin, we need to know that the success of which we speak is not statistical success. It is not a numbers game. It is not predicated on what others describe as success. Success in ministry is a combination of things. It is faithfulness mixed with care, effectiveness, and commitment to the Lord Jesus Christ. It is a mind-set that sees service as priority and servanthood as its conduit.

How does one celebrate success? What do you do when the blessings come and all seems right? How do you respond when your ministry seems to be on a roll?

*First,* celebrate. Honor the success, however large or small, in your heart. Acknowledge the moment. Give it a place in your memory, in your heart, in your history. Plant it there as a reminder of God's affirmation and blessing. Celebrate with family, with friends, with the church. Acknowledge to God that you are grateful and do not take His blessings for granted. Celebration of success is an appropriate part of our response to God.

*Second,* think positively. Guard against pessimism—don't wait for trouble to strike. Enjoy your success in ministry. Successful pastors do not fall prey to negative and reactionary influences. They seek the positive in every situation.

*Third,* plan for success. The great moments in ministry do not come simply with work and prayer. Success in any field is the by-product of planning. It is our way of bringing God into our thoughts and ministry. Paul talks about our "partnership in the gospel" (Phil. 1:5). We are encouraged to know that God has called us to be in "partnership" with Him in the greatest work in the world! Planning opens the heart and mind to the thoughts of God, to His way, and to His will.

*Fourth,* share your victories with your congregation. Celebrate the smallest success with your people. Remember—your celebration is an encouragement to your faithful supporters. Those who pray for you and with you deserve to know how God is blessing. When they hear the note of victory in the shepherd's voice, it is contagious. They are encouraged to expect future victories.

*Fifth,* keep a journal of God's work in your life and in the life of the church. One's history with God makes for great reading in the rough times. A journal is a reminder of God's blessings, how He helped in past situations, and His promises for the future. The pastor is a person of promise—God has called Him and promises His care and counsel. The One who calls is the One who says, "Never will I leave you; never will I forsake you" (Heb. 13:5).

*Sixth,* look for the tracks of God in your ministry. God leaves His heart print in the ministries of those whom He calls. He has a way of renewing His covenant with His followers. God has a way of involving himself in the ministry of His chosen. Successful pastors see the tracks of God, and they celebrate His presence, His blessings, and His affirmation of ministry.

*Seventh,* remember who you are in the journey of ministry. We are all redeemed persons, trying to be obedient to a call from God. We can earn no special favors from Him. Every success we have is a gift from His hand. We must remember our mission, our calling, and our goal. We are like the conductor on a passenger train who was making his last run before retirement. When a man asked him how he felt about his life as a conductor on a train, he replied, "It seems like I have spent my life trying to help people get home."[1] Our calling, our mission is to help people get home.

Gerald Kennedy wrote that he could never be out of debt to the past. He wrote, "There is no way to return to the older generations and return even a small part of what they have contributed to my welfare."[2] A part of our success is a contribution from someone. Our victories are not solo flights. Our lives are the resulting contributions of parents, family, friends, and teachers. Remember: who we are is to celebrate God's work in our ministry.

Enjoy your successes! God's call on your life is a call to grow, to succeed, to celebrate victories, and to enjoy the journey of ministry.

# *Notes*

**Chapter 1**
1. Mother Teresa, *Leadership,* fall 1989, 137.

**Chapter 2**
1. W. Raymond McClung, "Making a Difference," in *Sunrise Devotions* (Kansas City: Beacon Hill Press of Kansas City, 1991), 2:42.

**Chapter 3**
1. Marshall Shelley, *Leadership,* summer 1991, 3.

**Chapter 4**
1. Allan Cox, *Straight Talk for Monday Morning: Creating Values, Vision, and Vitality at Work* (New York: John Wiley and Sons, 1990), 295-96.

**Chapter 5**
1. Ernest Campbell, *Locked in a Room with Open Doors* (Dallas: Word Books, 1974), 34.

**Chapter 6**
1. Quoted in John C. Maxwell, *Be a People Person* (Wheaton, Ill.: Victor Books, 1989), 16.

**Chapter 7**
1. Don McCullough, "Waking from the American Dream," *Leadership* 10, No. 3 (summer 1990): 42.

**Chapter 10**
1. John Henry Jowett, *My Daily Meditation,* July 9 (La Verne, Calif.: El Camino Press, 1975), 195.
2. Ibid.

**Chapter 11**
1. H. B. London Jr. and Neil B. Wiseman, *Pastors at Risk* (Wheaton, Ill.: Victor Books, 1993), 30.
2. Eugene H. Peterson, *Working the Angles: A Trigonometry for Pastoral Work* (Grand Rapids: Wm. B. Eerdmans Publishing Co., 1987), 155.

**Chapter 12**
1. Stan Toler, *God Has Never Failed Me, but He's Sure Scared Me to Death a Few Times* (Tulsa, Okla.: Honor Books, 1995).
2. Quoted in Donna Fisher, *People Power* (Austin, Tex.: Bard and Stephen Publishers, 1995), 207.

3. John Walsh, "The Story Behind the Picture," *Guideposts*, September 1984, 3.

**Chapter 14**
1. Quoted in H. B. London Jr. and Neil B. Wiseman, *The Heart of a Great Pastor* (Ventura, Calif.: Regal Books, 1994), 22.
2. Ed Towne, *Leadership*, winter 1991, 57.
3. Herbert M. Carson, *Hallelujah!* (Hertfordshire, England: Evangelical Press, 1980), 74.
4. Craig Loscalzo, *Preaching Sermons That Connect* (Downers Grove, Ill.: InterVarsity Press, 1992), 77.
5. Dennis F. Kinlaw, *Preaching in the Spirit* (Wilmore, Ky.: Francis Asbury Press, 1985), 9.
6. Donald McCullough, Maxie Dunnam, Gordon MacDonald, "Enlarging the Mind to Expand the Ministry, Mastering Personal Growth," *Christianity Today*, 1992, 98.

**Chapter 15**
1. Jonathan G. Yandell, "Trust," *Leadership*, winter 1995, 39.

**Chapter 16**
1. Robert Callender, "Re-Focusing to Re-Empower a Ministry Gone Flat," *Journal of the American Academy of Ministry*, winter 1995, 5.
2. Quoted in Michael O'Donnell, *Home from Oz* (Dallas: Word Publishing, 1994), 159.
3. Max Lucado, *He Still Moves Stones* (Dallas: Word Publishing, 1993), 99.
4. Warren Wiersbe, *Something Happens When Churches Pray* (Wheaton, Ill.: Victor Books, 1984), 51.
5. John R. W. Stott, *Decision*, n.d.

**Chapter 17**
1. James Stewart, *Heralds of God* (New York: Charles Scribner's Sons, 1946), 47.
2. William Skudlarek, *The Word in Worship* (Nashville: Abingdon Press, 1981), 46.

**Chapter 18**
1. Lou Mobley and Kate McKeown, *Beyond IBM* (New York: McGraw-Hill Publishing Co., 1989), 30.

**Chapter 19**
1. Mobley and McKeown, *Beyond IBM*, 30.

**Chapter 21**
1. Dag Hammarskjöld, "Reflections," *Christianity Today*, July 19, 1994, 45.
2. Edward R. Dayton, *Succeeding in Business Without Losing Your Faith* (Grand Rapids: Baker Book House, 1992), 20.

110 PASTOR . . . BE ENCOURAGED

3. Ben Patterson, *Serving God* (Downers Grove, Ill.: InterVarsity Press, 1994), 168.

**Chapter 24**
1. Alex MacKenzie, *Time for Success* (New York: McGraw-Hill Publishing Co., 1988), 8.
2. Denis Haack, *The Rest of Success* (Downers Grove, Ill.: InterVarsity Press, 1989), 102-3.
3. Shelley Chapin, *Within the Shadow* (Wheaton, Ill.: Victor Books, 1991), 16.

**Chapter 25**
1. Gerald Kennedy, *Fresh Every Morning* (New York: Harper and Row, 1966), 174.
2. Ibid., 175.
3. Wesley Tracy, *What's a Nice God like You Doing in a Place like This?* (Kansas City: Beacon Hill Press of Kansas City, 1990), 83-84.

**Chapter 27**
1. David A. Seamands, *If Only* (Wheaton, Ill.: Victor Books, 1995), 14.
2. Alan E. Nelson, *Broken in the Right Place* (Nashville: Thomas Nelson, 1994), 11.
3. Richard A. Swenson, *Margin* (Colorado Springs: NavPress, 1992), 25.
4. Gordon MacDonald, *The Life God Blesses* (Nashville: Thomas Nelson, 1994), xiii-xiv.

**Chapter 28**
1. Warren Wiersbe, *On Being a Servant of God* (Nashville: Thomas Nelson, 1993), 14.

**Chapter 29**
1. Heidi Husted, "Four Ways I've Found Encouragement," *Leadership,* summer 1996, 44.
2. Kevin A. Miller, "From the Editor," *Leadership,* summer 1996, 3.
3. London and Wiseman, *Pastors at Risk*, 234.

**Chapter 30**
1. Charles L. Allen, *What I Have Lived By* (Old Tappan, N.J.: Revell, 1976), 117.
2. Gerald Kennedy, *The Parables* (New York: Harper and Row, 1960), 139.